PENGUIN BOOKS

SPIT IN THE OCEAN #7

KEN KESEY was born in 1935 and grew up in Oregon. He graduated from the University of Oregon and later studied at Stanford with Wallace Stegner, Malcolm Cowley, Richard Scowcroft, and Frank O'Connor. *One Flew Over the Cuckoo's Nest*, his first novel, was published in 1962. His second novel, *Sometimes a Great Notion*, followed in 1964. His other books include *Kesey's Garage Sale, Demon Box, Caverns* (with O.U. Levon), *The Further Inquiry, Sailor Song*, and *Last Go Round* (with Ken Babbs). His two children's books are *Little Tricker the Squirrel Meets Big Double the Bear* and *The Sea Lion*. Ken Kesey passed away on November 10, 2001.

ED MCCLANAHAN's friendship with Ken Kesey began in the early 1960s, when both were part of the Stanford community of writers. McClanahan's books include *The Natural Man, Famous People I Have Known*, and *Congress of Wonders*. He lives in Lexington, Kentucky.

All About Kesey

✳✳✳✳✳✳✳✳✳

Edited by

Ed McClanahan

PENGUIN BOOKS

PENGUIN BOOKS
Published by the Penguin Group
Penguin Group (USA) Inc., 375 Hudson Street,
New York, New York 10014, U.S.A.
Penguin Books Ltd, 80 Strand,
London WC2R 0RL, England
Penguin Books Australia Ltd, 250 Camberwell Road,
Camberwell, Victoria 3124, Australia
Penguin Books Canada Ltd, 10 Alcorn Avenue,
Toronto, Ontario, Canada M4V 3B2
Penguin Books India (P) Ltd, 11 Community Centre,
Panchsheel Park, New Delhi–110 017, India
Penguin Books (N.Z.) Ltd, Cnr Rosedale and Airborne Roads,
Albany, Auckland, New Zealand
Penguin Books (South Africa) (Pty) Ltd, 24 Sturdee Avenue,
Rosebank, Johannesburg 2196, South Africa

Penguin Books Ltd, Registered Offices:
80 Strand, London WC2R 0RL, England

First published in Penguin Books 2003

3 5 7 9 10 8 6 4 2

LIBRARY OF CONGRESS CATALOGING-IN-PUBLICATION DATA
Spit in the ocean #7 : all about Ken Kesey / edited by Ed McClanahan.
p. cm.
ISBN 0-14-200363-8
1. Kesey, Ken. 2. Authors, American—20th century—Biography. I. Title: Spit
in the ocean number 7. II. Title: Spit in the ocean number seven.
III. McClanahan, Ed.
PS3561.E667Z87 2003
813'.54—dc21
[B]   2003050439

Printed in the United States of America
Set in Bookman
Designed by Mia Risberg

CONTENTS

Grateful acknowledgment is made for permission to reprint the following copyrighted works:

"Haiku for Kesey" by Wavy Gravy. First appeared in *Rolling Stone*, issue of December 27, 2001–January 3, 2002. Reprinted by permission of the author and Rolling Stone LLC,

"Kesey's Last Prank" by Paul Krassner. First appeared in *High Times*, February 2002. Reprinted by permission of the author.

"Kentucky River Junction" from *Collected Poems: 1957–1982* by Wendell Berry. Copyright © 1985 by Wendell Berry. Reprinted by permission of North Point Press, a division of Farrar, Straus & Giroux, LLC.

"The Words on the Page" by Glen Love. First appeared under a different title in *The Eugene Register-Guard*, November 16, 2001. Reprinted by permission of the author.

"Stark Gets Off the Bus," an excerpt from "On the Road" by Larry McMurtry. First appeared in *The New York Review of Books*, December 5, 2002. Reprinted by permission of the author and *The New York Review of Books*.

"The Prankster Moves On" by John Daniel. First appeared in *Open Spaces Quarterly*. Reprinted by permission of the author.

"Last Go Round: A Song for Ken Kesey," words and music by Rosalie Sorrels. Copyright © 1995 by Grimes Creek Music. Used by permission of Rosalie Sorrels.

"The Day the Lampshades Breathed" from *Famous People I Have Known* by Ed McClanahan (Farrar, Straus & Giroux, 1985; University Press of Kentucky, 2003). Reprinted by permission of the author.

Illustrations on pages ix, 42, 89, 101, 108, 127, 139, and 232 by Doug Simon.

All other selections, with the exception of Ken Kesey's "Karma (and Other Sermons)" and "Earthshoes," are published for the first time in this volume and are the copyrighted properties of their respective authors.

Spit in the Ocean #7

Editor	Ed McClanahan
Associate Editor	Tom Marksbury
Assistant Editors	Ken Babbs
	Carolyn (Mountain Girl) Garcia
Art Editors	John Lackey
	Patrice Mackey
Artist-in-Residence	Doug Simon

Cohorts and collaborators: Darrin Branner-Rolat, Mark Chilton, Phil Deitz, Robert Faggen, Jonathan Greene, Mike Hagen, Ginger Jackson, Hilda McClanahan, Joe Petro III, John Witte, and Jim Wolpman. Special thanks to Ron "Hassler" Bevirt, who provided Prankster artifacts, good company, and Irish whiskey, and to Frivol, just for being wherever she is at any given moment.

For Kate, Caleb, and Jordan

HAIKU FOR KESEY

They say Kesey's dead—
but never trust a Prankster
even under ground
                    —*Wavy Gravy*

Among Gus Van Sant's many films is Even Cowgirls Get the Blues, *in which both Kesey and Ken Babbs make brief appearances. Van Sant's incandescent Polaroid of Kesey appeared in his collection* 108 Portraits *(Twin Palms Press, 1992). His film* Elephant *won the Palme d'Or at Cannes in 2003.*

SHAZAM!

A Foreword by Gus Van Sant

I first met Ken at his farm in the early 1980s, when I was a hired lighting man for a traveling BBC film documentary about LSD. Ken and I immediately bonded as fellow filmmakers. He was interested in the fledgling Portland film scene, of which I was a new member, having recently shot (but not finished) my first feature, a film called *Mala Noche.*

Ken was the original do-it-yourselfer (see the early issues of *Spit in the Ocean*), and he hoped to share what he had learned about filmmaking with other native Oregon filmmakers. It was an us-versus-them thing with him, the Oregonians valiantly battling the Hollywoodians. We were watching footage from the famous bus movie that he was editing on off-the-rack equipment—Sony, Motorola, regular VHS video gear that was really good, but didn't cost tens of thousands of dollars. The equipment itself, some of it painted Day-Glo, was exciting to him because it represented the low-cost tools the Oregon filmmakers were going to be using in their fight with the Hollywood establishment.

(As it turned out, Ken had it exactly right: That same equipment is what the kids nowadays favor over professional stuff to make their video movies. They call it pro-sumer, as opposed to consumer.)

I remembered that conversation years later, at Mason Williams's house in 1991, when once again we sat in front of a video monitor, watching bus footage. As we watched a sequence of the bus getting bogged down in a swamp, Ken grew weepy, and lifted his hands to dry his eyes. I said that it must be moving, watching some of that old footage. He said it wasn't the personal memories that made him tear up, but that "we lost the battle."

I said, "Well yeah, if that's the way you look at it, but it was a big battle . . . I mean, c'mon . . ."

"Well," he said, "we weren't playing to lose, we were playing to win. We knew we were playing a big game, and that's what makes me sad." Then, looking from me back to the monitor, he added, "We lost the big game."

I couldn't think of anything to say to that.

Around that same time, I took a picture of Ken on the back porch of his farmhouse as he looked out at the pond in the back yard. I had an old Polaroid camera with a lens that focused on its subject by means of an accordion bellows, which wheezed in and out as it focused. The sun was bright, the air was mellow. It was very quiet.

I clicked the shutter, ripped out the instant picture, and timed it for about a minute. Then I separated the picture from the gray, gooey secret-process backing, and we looked at the little black-and-white rectangle.

"What's that?" Ken said. "I guess I broke the camera."

There were jagged white rays coming out of Ken's head— probably some sort of aberration in the film, I thought, a defect of some kind. Ken posed for another one, but the results were the same, another flash of white-hot electricity emanating from his ear, this weird spidery electrical scratch. I tried a few more shots, but I couldn't get one clean picture without the lightning bolts leaping from Ken's head.

So we left it at that, a portrait with lightning bolts . . . not so bad. A week later I realized that there was a pinprick in the bellows of the camera, and the effect on Ken's picture, apparently, was the sun focusing itself through the pinhole precisely on Ken's noggin, drawing a picture of a lightning bolt as if it knew what it was doing, making a psychedelic quasar come out of the subject's head as he stood on a porch overlooking his irrigation pond and the woods behind his house.

✳✳✳✳✳✳✳✳✳✳✳✳✳✳✳✳✳✳✳✳✳✳✳✳

R.I.P.

SPIT IN THE OCEAN

1973–2003

An Introduction by Ed McClanahan

Spit in the Ocean was christened, according to my none-too-reliable recollection, one morning in 1973 in the kitchen of my house on Bryant Street in Palo Alto, which was a way station in those days for Prankster post-riders. Kesey and Babbs were there, of course, and (I think) Bobby Sky and Kathi Wagner and probably George Walker, all on their way back to Oregon from L.A. And I'm quite sure that Gordon Fraser, everybody's favorite local dealer, would have been there, too, because the Pranksters always needed refueling on these pit stops.

Anyhow, we were sitting around enjoying a tiny taste of Dr. Fraser's Rejuvenating Morning Pipe, and Kesey was talking about this magazine he was planning to publish up at the farm. There would be a total of seven issues, he said, and each issue would include one part of a seven-part serialized novel he intended to write, entitled *Seven Prayers by Grandma Whittier.* He would edit the first issue himself, Ken told me; it would feature matters having to do with aging, and its theme would be "Old in the Streets"—a play on a popular youth-cult movie of the day called *Wild in the Streets.* Then, he said, for each of the other six issues, there would be a different theme and a different editor—"kind of a wild-card editor," he added, thinking out loud. So far, it seemed, the magazine had no name.

Now as it happened, I had played a little penny-ante poker with Ken, and I knew that one of his favorite calls was the three-card-draw game called "Spit in the Ocean," wherein, as the dealer is doling out the cards, any one of the other players can holler "Spit!" at any given moment, upon which the dealer turns up the next card off the deck—let's say it's the eight of spades—and the rest of the eights automatically become wild cards. So . . .

"Hey!" I piped up (so to speak). "You oughta call it *Spit in the Ocean!*"

To tell the truth, I thought I was making a joke. But amazingly enough, here I am thirty years later, editing the seventh—and final—issue of a remarkably resilient little magazine by the name of . . . well, some folks calls it *SITO* for short, but I'm the goddamn editor this time, and I likes to call it *Spit*.

The first issue, Kesey's own "Old in the Streets," appeared in 1974. *Spit #2*, "Getting There from Here," came along in '76; its editor was the elusive, self-effacing New England investigative journalist who called himself simply "my." The third issue, "Communication with Higher Intelligence" (1977), was edited by my's opposite number, the flamboyant and notorious Dr. Timothy Leary, fresh out of prison at the time. Lee Marrs, the underground cartoonist, edited (and illuminated) *Spit #4*, the women's issue, "Straight from the Gut" (1978), and in '79 Richard and Elaine Loren took on #5, the "Pyramid Issue," which mostly consisted of Kesey's essay "The Search for the Secret Pyramid," previously serialized in *Rolling Stone*. *Spit #6*, Ken Babbs's "Cassady Issue" (1981), celebrated in fine style the life and high times of the late Neal Cassady, who almost alone bridged the gap between the Beat Generation and the Day-Glo Decade.

And in every issue, there was an episode of Kesey's *Seven Prayers by Grandma Whittier,* right on time.

But the endeavor was taking its toll. When I saw him in Oregon in the spring of '83, Ken allowed that he was pretty much burned out on the whole enterprise. Producing issue after issue of the magazine was burdensome enough—although he wasn't listed on the masthead, Ken was the de facto publisher from the first—and after the recent death of his own grandmother, who had been the model for the Grandma Whittier character, he had lost his enthusiasm for the novel as well, and was longing to get on with other writing projects, especially the collection of essays, quasi-fictional pieces, and poems that was to become, in 1986, *Demon Box*. After I got home to Kentucky, he wrote me to say that he'd about decided to give the magazine a rest, and heed the summons of his muse.

"I oughta drop this mind-slimin' belly-squeezin' mouth-parchin' SPITlessness," he wrote, "until the juices go to flowin' naturally. All the chemical primings just seem to further dry up the spring. . . ."

So here at last, after a twenty-two-year hiatus, is *Spit* #7, "All About Kesey."

It's both inevitable and fitting that this final issue of Ken's magazine should be a tribute to his genius, his vast energy, his generous humanity, and his imperturbable spirit. With that in mind, we've sought work with strong anecdotal content, writing that brings Kesey to the page alive and hale and shooting from the lip as only he could do—pieces like, for instance, the antic Paul Krassner's "Kesey's Last Prank," in which Ken becomes the resident poltergeist in Krassner's apartment. Or Lee Quarnstrom's luminous little gem, "A State of Grace." Or Kesey's own 1986 letter to his Kentucky writer friend Gurney Norman, about his misadventures in the Australian outback—and Norman's answer, equally rollicking, sixteen years later.

There's more, of course, much, much more: a revealing 1986 radio interview, never before in print; a pair of spirited poems by Montana cowboy poet Paul Zarzyski; a moving account of Ken's funeral by Sterling Lord, his literary agent for more than forty years; a lovely poem and letter by Kesey's (and Babbs's) Stanford classmate Wendell Berry; a fine essay by the Oregon poet and writer John Daniel; a stirring "Lament" by Grateful Dead lyricist Robert Hunter; contributions by such celebrated writers as Robert Stone, Tom Wolfe, Hunter S. Thompson, James Baker Hall, historian Douglas Brinkley, and

Larry McMurtry; all that plus a boatload—make that a bus-load—of recollections and reflections by old Prankster pals and many other friends, associates, and admirers. There are themes here, leitmotifs, an intricate web of connections and reconnections—Stanford, Oregon, the Dead, the Bus, Kentucky, Perry Lane, the West—with the legendary friendship of Kesey and Babbs a leitmotif unto itself. (Think Damon and Pythias, Butch and Sundance, Tom and Huck . . .)

And Kesey's own voice, as strong as ever, is heard throughout—in letters, in obscurely published or previously unpublished essays and speeches, and in two revealing interviews, in print here for the first time. Although he never revived the Grandma Whittier story, the editors would like to think there's still plenty in this volume to remind us all of the kind of writer, the kind of friend, and the kind of man Ken Kesey was.

While we were putting *Spit #7* together, someone suggested that we were making a sort of pointillist portrait, in which many small points of color and light come together to form the Big Picture. That reminded me of a portrait of George Washington I'd seen somewhere years ago, made up of hundreds of postage stamps, each of which bore a tiny portrait of . . . George Washington! This final issue of Ken's magazine aspires to add up in just that way—to constitute, in sum, an intimate, affectionate portrait of its founder, one which both honors him and bids him a fond farewell.

The expression "Sparks fly upward" was a natural favorite of Kesey's, suggesting as it does the soaring of the liberated spirit. He used it frequently both in private conversation and in addressing his larger public audience; it's even engraved on his headstone. But—as Ken would certainly have known—the line comes from the Book of Job (not ordinarily a source of sunny optimism), and it reads in its entirety, "Man is born into trouble, as sparks fly upward."

For all his ebullient disposition, Kesey knew more about trouble than most of us could bear—his and Faye's son Jed, twenty-one, was killed in a particularly ugly vehicular accident in 1984—and that terrible knowledge weighed heavily on him, and deepened him, I think, immeasurably. A few years ago, in a question-and-answer session, someone asked him, rather disdainfully, whether he "really believed" that acid offered the only path to enlightenment.

"Oh no," he answered, "grief will do it for you. But if I had a choice, I'd take acid every time."

Sparks fly upward.

A note on the text: The late Rumiocho, Ken's notoriously cantankerous macaw, apparently spelled his name several different ways; we settled for the variation in *Demon Box.* No passionate defenders of "Hoo Haw" or "Hoo-Hah" materialized, so we went with Hoo-Ha. As to Furthur vs. Further, we decided to leave that delicate distinction up to the writers—and to you.

Michael Strelow is the editor of Kesey, *a compendium of* Kesiana *published by* Northwest Review *in 1977, which will soon be re-issued by the University of Oregon Press. Strelow now teaches at Williamette University in Salem, Oregon. Photos by Clyde Keller.*

ALL THAT HOO-HA

By Michael Strelow

William S. Burroughs had recently come out of some kind of rehab and arrived at Kesey's (after a layover at the Naropa Institute in Colorado) just as the First Perennial Poetic Hoo-Ha was in its opening stages. It was June of 1976 at the Kesey barn-house near Pleasant Hill, Oregon. Burroughs looked nervous and out of place in the panorama of barns and ponds, a city guy dreaming of a nightmare country. Kesey and a small entourage walked Burroughs out to show him the new blueberry bushes planted over about an acre of landscape pocked with surreal apricot-colored mounds of sawdust with scrawny bushes poking up. There were many big birds around the place—guinea hens, a macaw, peacocks, chickens, and others—and one of them, a bull peacock dragging his tail, followed along behind the group, maybe hoping for a feed. Kesey and Burroughs were side by side in the lead, each with a glass of whiskey in hand, Burroughs in a gray suit with narrow lapels, a thin black tie, and pants a good four inches above his shoes, Kesey showing his guest through his new agricultural project. The peacock, as if something had pierced its heart, suddenly let out with a single sharp, strident yip, offering up all its life in one woeful shriek. Burroughs started violently and somehow launched the contents of his glass straight up, amber whiskey and ice cubes hanging for a second against the blue sky, then dropping back into the glass like a party trick. Burroughs, after a moment, offered a quick sniff and a slight shudder, and the walk continued as if nothing could astound in this landscape, as if nothing at all out of the ordinary had just happened.

There was a teepee just visible over the hill beyond the fishpond. Some thin man walked through the grass wearing only what looked to be a diaper. A pack of kids raced around the barn and disappeared like a string of ponies. A load of poets from Santa Cruz piled out of a dusty car—lots of poets from a very small car, like circus clowns. Two lay down immediately in the grass. There were rumors that Dylan would show up; Burroughs already had.

Burroughs and Portland poet Marty Christiansen

Inside, on a shelf near the designated kitchen area, was a World War II field telephone in an olive-drab box with a two-handed receiver. Ken Babbs was on the phone jabbering in a German accent, in which the words "panzer" and "Rommel" were clearly distinguishable. It seemed you had to yell into the phone to be heard, and the German accent floated over the top of the twenty or so milling people in the house: poets, reporters, a spoon player, various friends, sycophants, and gawkers, a few neighbors in overalls washed to near whiteness, University of Oregon M.F.A. students, and a group I could never figure out apparently consisting of lower-echelon Merry Pranksters who followed the wackiness at some distance.

The eating and drinking never seemed to stop, as if the festivities had tapped into some inexhaustible supply of hunger and thirst beneath the hills of Pleasant Hill, Oregon. Toward evening the visitors thinned out. There was a bonfire away from the buildings, and it looked like any evening at summer camp. Faye Kesey seemed always to be gazing over the top of the activity, undisturbed, with a detachment steeped in years of observing high jinks and folderol. She seemed to be enjoying it all. Ken never slowed. He had hatched the Hoo-Ha, and was now tending it, whatever it was. The rubric was this: What is the pelt of art worth? And ITSART—Intrepid Trips Society for Aesthetic Revolutionary Training—was the production company in charge of asking the question.

All day Saturday the Hoo-Ha itself formed as a running paper fence across the UO athletic fields around McArthur Court. Colored markers were available in boxes, and poets of all manner, description, variety, and vintage—students, Deadheads, city council members, escapees from a high school field trip—were industriously filling the Hoo-Ha with poems and words of wisdom. There were people squatting along the paper fence reading what was written, others writing more, kids playing tag in and out of the breaks in the fence that let people flow from one side to the other. All afternoon the crowd built up, milling along the fence, and although no one knew exactly what was going on, everyone seemed pleased to write into the huge poem that, by evening, covered both sides of the fence.

Portland poet Walt Curtis and Paul Krassner

Then Saturday night, with Mac Court filled to the seven- or eight-thousand mark, Kesey, Babbs, and crew emcee-ing like a succession of Ed Sullivans announcing the acts: spoon player, Santa Cruz poet, Anne Waldman ("fast talking woman" poet from New York), Burroughs, local poet, spoon player, spoon player. After a while, the spoon player sat with legs hanging over the edge of the stage, ready to fill in as necessary, because the acts came out of the green room slower and slower until it seemed the spoon guy sat like the stage manager in *Our Town*, commenting with the clack of his spoons on all that occurred. The green room was having its own Hoo-Ha, parallel to the public one. Anne Waldman left in a huff over what was rumored to be an ass-patting incident involving an unnamed Santa Cruz poet. Venerable Mac Court was fragrant with grass, and in the darkened balconies up near the ceiling flared temporary stars of lighting and relighting, as somewhere the fire marshal shuddered.

The name "Hoo-Ha" referred, variously, to the whole event including months of planning, to the white paper fence begging for the language of the tribe to be written on it, and finally to any gesture or remembrance or comment on the event, including the perpetually evanescent. It was manufactured life much like the fabled bus trip; it was confirmation and data for the general and insatiable data banks of all forms and manifestations of Prankster.

I found myself there by occupation and nature and inclination. I was the editor of the literary magazine *Northwest Review*, and between editing the magazine and Ph.D. classes and a family there came the Hoo-Ha (the first one; by the time the second one came along I knew what I was getting into, and stayed a little lower in the whole scheme of things).

The first time I met Ken Kesey, I had called him to ask if I could assemble a book out of the boxes of his literary papers that he had given to the University of Oregon library. I had gone through the papers looking for a way to contrive a book that showed the sources of *One Flew Over the Cuckoo's Nest* and *Sometimes a Great Notion.* What looked like a fine dust on the papers was really dried chicken shit; they had been stored on the bus for a while, and the chickens had sought literary roosts. When I began to work with the papers, my eyes began immediately to itch and burn, and I sneezed and sneezed and sneezed. I would wash my hands and face, go sit in the sun until the burning stopped, then try it again. And I soon became convinced that there was great stuff there (eventually the book *Kesey*); I only needed to get Kesey's permission to proceed.

Someone picked me up at the university bookstore in a gray Cadillac convertible for the ride out to Pleasant Hill. Ken's sister-in-law Sue Kesey (she ran the Springfield Creamery with her husband, Chuck) was along. Within a few months she and I would be the designated logicians trying to parse out the requirements of time and space for the Hoo-Ha.

At the barn-house, there was a poster-sized rendition of a William Blake illustration filled in with Day-Glo colors on one wall. The whole living room floor was taken up by a deep-red wrestling mat, and a ring of theater seats seemed to seal off the exits, with some seats up and some down like missing teeth. I had no idea what to expect, because what I had expected, a serious talk about copyright, proper credits for the book, etc., vanished as I went inside. My book business clearly took second place to the heavy literary discussion already in progress. I remember some of it:

". . . and then the Bible."

"New Testament."

"Definitely New Testament."

"Matthew. Mark. Luke . . ."

"John. Definitely John. Oh yes, John. Maybe only John."

"Yes, John. John. Not John the Divine. Just plain John."

I suppose I shared bafflement with lots of people new to the Prankster ways. John Clark Pratt, in his introduction to the Viking Critical Library edition of *Cuckoo's Nest* ("On Editing Kesey: Confessions of a Straight Man"), documents the O.D. field telephone and required German accent there, too. But I remember thinking the craziness level wasn't much beyond the standard graduate school get-together—maybe a few more props, a little more of a center around the whirling figure of Kesey. So I waited through the Blake poster, the endless snacks as if no one had eaten in days.

Indeed, much of my early Hoo-Ha contact with Kesey seemed to be fueled by one food or another. A few weeks later, Wavy Gravy, who had been at the coast, came back with coolers full of Dungeness crabs. Kesey called people to come help eat them. Bring beer. The Blake poster was gone, but there were new puppies. Something going on, something happening in Pleasant Hill.

I was writing my dissertation on Emerson, and maybe that had something to do with it. I thought the group gatherings near Mount Pisgah in Pleasant Hill seemed a natural extension of the transcendental-related communes of Brook Farm and Fruitlands of the 1840s. The finding of the self, Emerson's "great and crescive self," by good people coming together with good intentions, informed much of the American nineteenth-century social experiments: Oneida Colony, Amana Society, New Harmony, North American Fourierist Phalanx, Hutterites, Owenites. The Merry Pranksters, charismatic leader in place (its John Humphrey Noyes, Robert Owen, Bronson Alcott), was about seeking the worth of the self, turning on the self to itself through experience. The Hoo-Ha (and the bus trip and the Bend in the River political meetings of the early 1970s) constituted a temporary alliance of people of all sorts to see what would happen.

Ken Kesey was a genius at getting things to occur around him, getting life to intensify for the Hoo-Ha over months of preparations/meetings/parties—jacked-up discussions of everything in general and, for the Hoo-Ha, literary arts in particular, and what the pelt was worth. Who cared about what. Who would pay what to be in the presence of whom. Could this thing support itself for more years? Who could be seduced by the long communal poem that was a Hoo-Ha?

The lights in Mac Court were turned to minimum and people were nearly done filing out into the Oregon spring night. My final job was to empty all the ashtrays with a net scoop that strained the sand for butts; if we didn't do this, the University would charge us extra to have it done. The big doors were open to the outside, and the night air felt good. All that poetry and spoon-playing had cooked the air inside into a roux. The pelt of art had somehow been brought in and nailed to the wall in one night of poetry, fiction, and nonfiction—and spoons. The whole impression of the show was informed by the clackety-clack of the spoons that had clattered around all those words, all that Hoo-Ha.

In the late 1950s Kesey and James Wolpman, a young attorney, became neighbors and friends on Perry Lane, a small bohemian community near Stanford University, where both were students. In the 1960s Wolpman was one of the founders of the Law Commune, a Palo Alto collective of activist lawyers. Later a judge in the California legal system, he has recently retired, and now lives in Walnut Creek. Kesey's letter to him was written in late 1968 or early '69.

✳✳✳✳✳✳✳✳✳✳✳✳✳✳✳✳✳✳✳✳✳✳✳✳

A LETTER TO JIM WOLPMAN

By Ken Kesey

Jim:

A long overdue letter to say first, thanks, and next I'm not sure what. Let's see . . .

What do I think about it all at this point? My mind is cloudy about R_____ L_____—no, smokey is more ~~kw~~ what it is; sulfuric-bu~~yx~~

I feel newly clear about the revolution, which is our true common ground anyway, so I'll ramble about that. I believe, as Burroughs put it in I think The Soft Machine, that the Third World War is now being fought in the space between our cells. It is a battle over territory, turf, over who gets to shout WUXTRA on the prime corner, over whether the rich loam riverside land down by the ~~lax~~ Jasper Bridge is used to raise vegitables or whether Cantells are forced by rising property taxes and seductive offers to sell to the trailer housers.

10

Okay, for the sake of argument, lets say the trailer-housers are the bad guys, or at least in the employ of the bad guys! These are the strip-miners, the ghetto makers, the conspirators; dolts, really, for they will be sold out by the conspiracy. As you read the new Realist you realise that even Nixon will be sold out by the conspiracy.

So it seems to me that the trick is how to keep from selling out as ~~Skt~~ the squeeze increases and the opportunities burgeon.

Why couldn't McGovern stick by Eagleton, or John Wayne by Goldwater for that matter? What makes us sell out? My theory is that it isn't money, or power, or even glory; its because we are all still in high school and more than anything else in the world we want to be considered a Regular Fellow. And we are coerced more than anything else by the ~~Shooghtzmf~~ fear of having to sit alone at the edge table in the caffeteria at noon hour and hear all the real, regular Regular Fellows at another table guffawing and sniggering; and glancing in our direction as they whisper to each other. O, to be at that table, socked securely in the bosom of brotherhood, be it black, bearded, Ivy league buttondown or just a bunch of boys whooping it up!

O to be gazed upon with such worship by the table full of yell queens in voluminous letter-men's sweaters! O to be in with the In Crowd (I know a lot of people who don't believe they've really experienced an orgasm without they read about it in Rolling Stone), to swing with the Swingers, to click with the clique!

It's our drama, our generation's hang-up trying to unravel itself before we are strangled on moldy old crepe streamers leading all the way back to the Junior Prom.

It's what Carnal Knowledge is about, and Summer of '42, and Play it Again Sam, and, mainly, bestly: The Last Picture Show. Larry is trying to dig back and unfuse that bomb we all had a hand in wiring up back in high school, so that us Regular Fellows can communicate with the Yell Queens we married without the communication being filtered through rolls in an awful coven, so the coven may be dispersed and its power over us debunked, so we can become men and women to each other and tell the makers of Right Guard and Pristine to shove it up their ass.

Now, on these terms, let's examine the three as of us.

Did we behave like revolutionaries? Forgetting all that went on before and bringing it right down to that big redwood table, I say we all three did good. Ed was there, a Regular Fellow to us all, but we did not play to him. In fact, R_____ L_____ might have taken the Che Award that morning (he had the most to gain in the Regular Ranks; me and you already being heavies and him like the new kid come in from out of state in the middle of the term) with his hardheaded refusal to kowtow . . . if it had not been for that one slight stammer when we played the tape back. That lost him the coveted "Guevara" but even so he was even up with you and I at the end and we're no slouches!

Anyway, thanks again. Not for your judgment about who won the race, but for the pace you set. You not only kept a mud bath from becoming a blood bath you even managed to clean things up a bit.

Paul Krassner is the political satirist whose magazine The Realist *was a thorn in the side of the body politic for more than forty years. He is also a stand-up comedian, with two CDs to his credit. His latest collection of satirical essays and social commentary is* Murder at the Conspiracy Convention; *it includes a longer version of "Kesey's Last Prank," which first appeared in* High Times *in February 2002.*

KESEY'S LAST PRANK

By Paul Krassner

On the mantel over the fireplace stood my personal icon, a papier maché Donald Duck with eight arms. But on this particular day, there was something vaguely different about him. Then I realized what it was. He now had ten arms. The additional arms were actually two pairs of shoelaces. Ken Kesey had been around. He had purchased a pair of shoelaces for himself, but they only came in packages of three. Such a prank was Kesey's way of showing affection.

In late October 2001, surgeons cut out 40 percent of his liver, but the remaining scarred-up hunk-o-meat wasn't in such good shape either, extremely cirrhotic, plus diabetes and hepatitis C. On the morning of November 10, if you clicked on a headline, "Kesey Recovers from Cancer Surgery," on msn.com, you would have learned that he had died. Oh, if only this had been just another prank. But no, the culture had lost a novelist and folk hero, and I had lost a fine friend.

In February 1971, publisher Stewart Brand invited Kesey

and me to co-edit *The Last Supplement to the Whole Earth Catalog*. Kesey was seated in a Palo Alto backyard at a table with an electric typewriter. His parrot, Rumiocho, was perched on a tree limb right above him, and whenever Rumiocho squawked, Kesey would type a sentence as though the parrot were dictating to him. Kesey looked up. "Hey, Krassner, I've just been sitting here, thinking about the anal sphincter."

By the magic of coincidence, I reached into my pocket, withdrew a piece of printed wisdom that had traveled 3,000 miles with me when I moved from New York to San Francisco. It was titled "The Anal Sphincter: A Most Important Human Muscle." I handed it to Kesey and said, "My card." It was a most auspicious new beginning.

Each morning, Kesey and our managing editor, Hassler (his Prankster name), would come to the Psychodrama Commune where I was staying. We'd all have crunchy granola and ginseng tea. Then, sharing a joint in an open-topped convertible, we'd drive along winding roads sandwiched by forest, ending up at a huge garage filled with production equipment. Kesey and I would discuss ideas, pacing back and forth like a pair of caged foxes. Gourmet meals were cooked on a potbellied stove. Sometimes a local rock band came by and rehearsed with amplification that drowned out the noise of our typewriters.

Kesey had been reading a book of African Koruba stories. The moral of one parable was "He who shits in the road will meet flies on his return." With that as a theme, we assigned R. Crumb to draw his version of the Last Supper for our cover of *The Last Supplement*.

One morning at breakfast, I couldn't help but notice that Kesey had taken a box from the pantry and was pouring some white powder from it into his crotch. "I've used cornstarch on my balls for years," he explained. It sounded like an organic commercial in the making. Our public service ad would appear with step-by-step photos on the inside back cover of the Supplement—which, after all, was about tools, information, ideas, and visions—with Kesey giving this pitch:

"I know how it is when you're swarthy anyway and maybe nervous like on a long freeway drive or say you're in court where you can't unzip to air things out, and your clammy old nuts stick to your legs? Well, a little handful of plain old cornstarch in the morning will keep things dry and sliding the

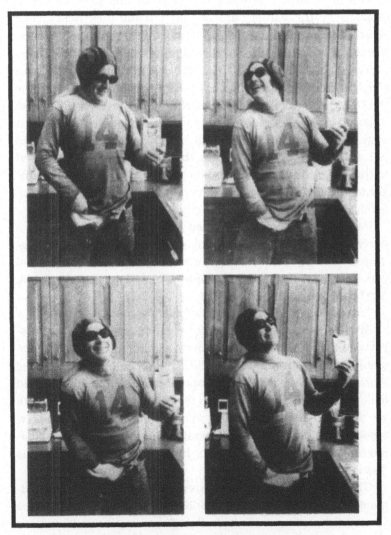

"I've used Cornstarch on my balls for years!"

whole hot day long. Works better than talcum and you don't smell like a nursery. Also good for underarms, feet, pulling on neoprene wet suits and soothing babies' bottoms. And it's biodegradable."

One afternoon, two black women from Jehovah's Witnesses stopped by the garage, and within ten minutes Kesey convinced them that in Revelations, where there's talk of locusts, it was really a reference to helicopters. Kesey threw the I Ching every day as a religious ritual. When his daughter Shannon was invited out on her first car date, he insisted that she throw the I Ching in order to decide whether or not to accept. Once he forgot to bring his family I Ching to the garage, and he seemed edgy, like a woman who had neglected to take her birth-control pill, so I suggested that he pick three numbers, then I turned to that page in the unabridged dictionary, circled my index finger in the air, and it came down pointing at the word *bounce*. So that was our reading, and we bounced back to work.

After two months we finished the Supplement and had a party. Somebody brought a tank of nitrous oxide. Kesey suggested that in cave-dwelling times, all the air they breathed was like this. "There are stick figures hovering above," he said, "and they're laughing at us."

"And," I added, "the trick is to beat them to the punch."

We hung around La Honda for a while. Kesey had once discovered a tunnel inside a cliff overlooking the beach. We were smoking hash in the tunnel, which had been burrowed during World War II so that military spotters with binoculars could look toward the ocean's horizon for oncoming enemy ships. All we spotted was a meek little mouse in the tunnel. We blew smoke at that mouse until it could no longer tolerate our behavior. The mouse stood on its hind paws and roared at us *"Squeeeeeeekk!"*

This display of mouse assertiveness startled us, and we almost fell off the cliff. The headline would have read, "Dope Crazed Pranksters in Suicide Pact." And it all would've been One-Legged Terry's fault.

A few years later, I was sharing an apartment with Stewart Brand. On the wall of my room I taped a photo of my daughter Holly and two posters: President Nixon, whom I disdained; and a Native American, Geronimo, whom I admired.

One evening I sensed that there was something vaguely different in my room.

Then I realized what it was—my Richard Nixon poster. His eyes, which had always looked toward the right, were now looking toward the left. It had that eerie effect of the Jesus-face plaque in a novelty-shop window, where his eyes would follow you as you passed. Except that Nixon's eyes were frozen in this position.

I examined the poster more closely and was able to discern that the original eyeballs had been whited out from the right side, and new eyeballs had been drawn in the left-hand corners. Then I checked to see whether the eyes in Holly's photo had also been changed, but she was still looking directly at me. So was my Indian guide. Only Nixon's eyes had been altered. It seemed out of character for Stewart to have done this, but I asked him anyway.

"No, it wasn't me," he said. "But Kesey was around for a while."

Of course! I should've realized it was Kesey when I saw that telltale trail of cornstarch.

There are those who would like to imagine Kesey on That Great Bus in the Sky, with Cassady at the wheel and Garcia on the guitar and Leary on acid, but everybody remembers him in their own way. When his little grandson learned of Kesey's death, he asked, "But now who will teach us how to hypnotize the chickens?"

Patrice Mackey, his wife, Jennifer Jewett, and their daughters Sofia and Isabel live in Eugene. A computer technologist, a gourmet chef, and an ardent music collector, he has long been a mainstay of the annual Burning Man festival, where he is known as Chef Juke.

IT'S THE KIDS

By Patrice Mackey

11/15/2001

So I just spent a day mourning, celebrating, and helping bury this unusual friend of mine, Ken.

I saw his other friends and family. We hugged each other. We wept together. We joked together. We shook our fists with anger at our friend for leaving us too soon.

66 years old. 24,161 days and nights.

Too few.

I figured out that I knew him for about 4,736 of those days and nights.

Still too few.

While he certainly was famous . . . I knew him outside of that fame. I knew him as a father to his kids, a grandfather to Caleb, Jordan, and Kate, and a beloved surrogate uncle to my two kids.

The kids.

It's the kids, I think, who will miss him the most. The grown-ups he knew had a chance to experience him time and again. Each of his kids, nieces, and nephews has a million stories they could tell about how great he was to play with when they were growing up. But the grandkids only got a glimpse.

When the pallbearers carried his tie-dyed coffin out of the theater where the public memorial was held, my nine-year-old, Sofia, broke into uncontrollable sobs. Ken's mom, Geneva, had been holding up pretty well until then, but when she saw Sofia she broke down too. When my four-year-old, Isabel, heard that he had died, she went to the kitchen table and came back five minutes later with a picture. She said, "This is Caleb and Jordan crying 'cause they miss their granddad."

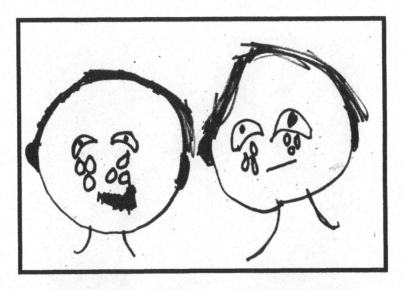

Ken was a writer, a performer, a prankster, a hardheaded sonofabitch, and a lot of other things. He was famous for many of them. But if you wanted to see this man at his best, it was with children.

Once, at an event at the Fillmore in San Francisco, the "Psychedelic-Era Reunion Party," he saw Sofia (then about five) in the crowd and went right over to her and took her hand and walked around admiring the scene with her. When the photographers asked him to come over to the "posing area" for a shot, he and Sofia walked over and sat down together. When one of the photographers said, "Little girl, could you move over so we could get a picture of Ken?" you would have thought he had asked Ken to cut off his right arm. Ken was incensed at him for suggesting that Sofia should move an inch just so this guy could get a "better" shot. He only said a few words to him, but the message was clear: She doesn't have to move an inch. You can take a picture or not. That's up to you. The photographer shrunk down to about fourteen inches tall and backed off right away. He was quickly replaced by the noted rock photographer Jay Blakesberg, who took this picture:

© 2003 by Jay Blakesberg

So it's the kids I feel the most for. Ken was a purveyor of wonder. Some audiences he had to work pretty hard to show them that wonder. Kids, I think, were easier. Either way, when he hit you with it, it stayed with you.

I've spent the last few days reading every one of the 1,945

e-mail messages that have been sent to his website. I've watched the visit counter roll on past 50,000 hits since Saturday morning when he passed on. I've read how he's touched people who never came within 1,000 miles of meeting him and still were profoundly moved by something he wrote, something he did, or something they'd only heard that he did.

It's not a lot of people who can move so many that way.

I'm gonna miss that guy.

Douglas Brinkley is director of the Eisenhower Center for American Studies and professor of history at the University of New Orleans. He is currently writing a biography of Jack Kerouac.

MAJIC BUS MEETS FURTHER II

By Douglas Brinkley

Ken Kesey's Willamette Valley Farm is out of the way, address-free, and not particularly easy to find. But as Ralph Waldo Emerson wrote, "If a man can write a better book, preach a better sermon, or make a better mouse trap than his neighbor, though he build his house in the woods, the world will beat a path to his door." In 1992, I brought a group of eighteen college students from Hofstra University to meet this famed Oregon dairy farmer best known for writing such enduring classics as *One Flew Over the Cuckoo's Nest* and *Sometimes a Great Notion.* We were crisscrossing America in my "Majic Bus," a classroom on wheels whose mission was to study American history, literature, and culture in a hands-on fashion. Kesey, I knew, was many things to many people: novelist of unusual force, accomplished magician, fireside storyteller, creative writing instructor at the University of Oregon, popularizer of tie-dye clothing and Day-Glo colors, ringleader of the psychedelic sixties, college wrestler turned wrestling coach, carnival showman, outlaw legend. He was the man who threw a party in San Francisco and saw half of America show up.

The Kesey persona that had drawn the Majic Bus to his

Pleasant Hill doorstep was that of Kesey the catalyst, the last wagon master, the innovative unsettler who with his band of Merry Pranksters helped trigger a revolution of consciousness in the 1960s with his notorious 1939 International Harvester bus Furthur. The grapevine had informed me that Kesey now had a successor bus, named Further (or Further II). I was hoping Kesey might take my Majic Bus students for a ride.

Besides *One Flew Over the Cuckoo's Nest*, I had assigned Tom Wolfe's best-selling *Electric Kool-Aid Acid Test*, an account of the maiden transcontinental journey of Kesey and thirteen of the Merry Pranksters, in preparation for meeting him. In 1964, the giddy band traversed America from California to New York in a psychedelic painted bus exploring the mind-expanding wonders of LSD. Behind the wheel was none other than counterculture folk hero Neal Cassady, the model for Dean Moriarty in Jack Kerouac's *On the Road*. Wolfe chronicled the wanderings of "the Hieronymus Bosch bus . . . with the destination sign in front reading 'Furthur' and a sign in back saying 'Caution: Weird Load.'" But as journalist Paul Perry and Prankster Ken Babbs pointed out in their book, *On the Bus*, this most infamous and riotous transcontinental bus trek ever was an event of immense historical and cultural importance, for "the torch had been passed from the Beat to the Psychedelic, with Cassady as the driver, the tour guide, the swing man, foot in both eras, the flame passing from Kerouac to Kesey."

By 1992 the psychedelic sixties were being viewed with that certain historical detachment that time eventually accords to all eras, no matter how tumultuous. In 1990 the Smithsonian's National Museum of American History, for example, sought to purchase the original Furthur from Kesey. "It is not a typical bus," said a museum public-affairs officer. "Its historical context is important for what it meant to the literary world of a certain generation." The only trouble was that Furthur was defunct, rusting and rotting away on Kesey's Oregon farm, covered with moss and spiderwebs, in a state of complete moldering disrepair, impossible to rebuild. Instead of informing the Smithsonian of Furthur's demise, Kesey, his Pranksterism having survived the eighties intact, bought a similar 1949 version of the bus. With his son Zane and several Prankster friends, among others, he went to work refurbishing and repainting this successor, bringing it to a high sheen of Day-Glo glory.

The prank was to palm off the simulation as the original for the unsuspecting Smithsonian to display. Besides the thick layers of Day-Glo paint and psychedelic doves, clouds, shooting stars, and squiggles that cover Further II, Kesey added some fresh interior touches: Dada collages and photo clippings of personalities ranging from Kerouac to Einstein to Ella Fitzgerald, and above the wheel a large drawing of Neal Cassady, the psychedelic Saint Christopher of the American Highway. Kesey transferred Cassady's driver's seat, an authentic relic from the original bus, into Further II to maintain continuity with the Beat days past. A small bronze statue of a court jester, a jokerman, became the hood ornament. Beanbag chairs and sofa cushions were scattered about the floor, making the interior an unlikely misalliance between a bourgeois living room and a traveling opium den. Beyond listing such details, the only way to describe Further II was as a kaleidoscope of explosive colors, a Day-Glo fireworks display on wheels, a rainbow-sherbet swirl of every color under the sun, and then some. The Grateful Dead donated a high-powered stereo system for the bus and Kesey traded in his reel-to-reels for CDs. He enlisted an adventurous crew largely comprised of former Pranksters and younger soulmates, inviting them to cross the continent. In Washington, D.C., they would help pass off Further II as the real McCoy at a Smithsonian ceremony—where, who knew, maybe the fruit punch might get laced.

In November of 1990, Kesey and company took to the road, stopping at shopping malls and roadside restaurants, bringing smiles to the lips of the locals. They hit San Francisco for a dose of nostalgia, cruising past Longshoremen's Hall, site of the infamous Trips Festival of January 1966, where the Pranksters and others inaugurated what became the first strobe light and acid-rock show. They passed Golden Gate Park and the meadow where the Summer of Love Be-ins were held, and headed to (you guessed it) the Haight-Ashbury district. All the while, the Dead's new sound system was blasting the Grateful Dead and Bob Dylan's "Mr. Tambourine Man," causing necks to crane, cyberpunks to give the thumbs-up, and college-age Deadheads to beg for a spin.

Kesey wanted to show a new generation of Americans that despite death and divorce and personal disasters, the Prankster spirit survived—that, in his words, they had made good on a promise. "We have to reestablish the whole idea of trust in the nation," Kesey declared at a Further II rally in Berkeley. "The war is not on drugs, it's on consciousness. If Jesse Helms wants to lock horns with God, I can take him up there and introduce him in twenty minutes. But it won't be the Southern Baptist God with the big voice and the white beard; it'll be the God of the stars and the lights and the planets and the colors."

A few days after the rally, Kesey's bus was shanghaied in Stockton, California, stolen by Zane and some of the younger crew, and driven back to Oregon. On the pavement where the bus had stood, Kesey found a chalked outline of Further and a simple inscription of the Prankster motto: "Nothing lasts." Kesey had been outpranked by his son. Zane's message was that Further II was alive and running and didn't belong in a museum. Kesey returned home, and he ensconced the new bus in his barn, to be called into service on special occasions or when the spirit moved.

As my Majic Bus left I-5 and headed down Highway 58 in a misty fog to the small town of Pleasant Hill, all of my students' eyes were peeled for a Dairy Queen, the landmark at which Kesey had instructed us to turn left. Speculation was rampant as to whether Kesey would take us for a spin in the new Further. I volunteered that I thought it was unlikely—best to keep expectations low. Besides our being hours late, the skies were gray, indicating rain was imminent. I surmised we would sit around and talk about *One Flew Over the Cuckoo's Nest* and Neal Cassady, eat some potato chips and pretzels, and leave.

Finally we spotted the Dairy Queen, turned left, and followed a curvy country road past brown, moon-eyed cows and ranch-style homes with lawns sprouting a thousand varieties of green vegetation—until we saw a white star painted in a bright blue circle on the side of a red barn: We recognized Kesey's homestead. Our excitement mounted at the sight of a yellow road sign with a black silhouette of a kangaroo on it—a warning that we were entering the uncharted kingdom of Keseyland.

As we cleared some low-hanging tree branches and turned up the dirt driveway, the students caught their first glimmering of Kesey's predilection for bright colors: a family of peacocks showboating and strutting about the place, their piercing cries announcing our arrival. Anticipation was running high. My students could scarcely believe they were about to meet the cultural warrior of the sixties whose legendary Merry Prankster antics they had heard about for years, from aging hippies at Dead concerts or from "weird, trippy" uncles who had taken Scott MacKenzie's musical advice and headed to San Francisco.

When we got out of the bus, there was Ken Kesey with his son Zane (who was running Key-Z Productions), all smiles and hearty handshakes, keenly interested in whether his directions had been sufficient. Wearing a darkish blue jumpsuit over a tie-dyed shirt, a hay straw in his mouth and a navy blue sailor's cap—the kind Jack London used to wear—on his head, Kesey looked forty, not fifty-six, being possessed of both the silveriness of Paul Newman and the beefy demeanor of Gene Hackman. "Come on inside," he offered, "we've got some hot dogs and beans ready for you all." Kesey knew how to win over young people's hearts—food. With nothing in their stomachs, save a roadside breakfast snack, they dug in with a vengeance. We were chowing down in a psychedelic version of Pee Wee's Playhouse—posters of Wavy Gravy, the Dead, and Neal Cassady hung on the rustic walls, and a giant ball of hemp twine lay stationary on the floor. Day-Glo paint covered everything, from Kesey's suitcase to his dog's tail.

It was amazing to watch his famed charisma at work.

Within minutes he had captivated the students with charming stories and an irresistible smile. "Hurry up and eat," Kesey prompted, "we've got pretty good weather and enough daylight hours to take Further out for a spin." We all gulped in disbelief. Had he said we were taking Further for a spin? Kesey opened a closet and began pulling out Day-Glo jumpsuits for us to wear, as well as crazy hats—including one with fuzzy brown bear ears. It was really happening. We were going to drive around the Oregon countryside with Ken Kesey's foot on the accelerator.

Suitably attired, we followed Kesey and Zane out to the bus barn. Sure enough, there was Further II, a rebellion in color, an affirmation of life. While Kesey got the bus road-ready, some of us walked back past a murky pond filled with springtime bullfrogs to a mossy grove of trees where an old wooden fishing boat called "Deeper" was rotting away, decomposing, becoming one with nature once more. With trees drooling moss and a chorus of croaking frogs, it felt more like the Louisiana bayou than rural Oregon. Near the boat lay the original Furthur, like a fallen warrior still recognizable as a bus, with a cardboard skeleton sitting approximately where Neal Cassady once sat. The paint job was more Picassoesque and less Pollackian than I had imagined. The famed roof bubble still gave the bus a futuristic aura, though the glass was now opaque from twenty-five years of grime. As we jogged back to the barn, not wanting to be left behind while the others went on the ride of a lifetime, we noticed that almost every yard object had been transfigured with a bit of Day-Glo—an electric pink hose or chain, a blue ax or a yellow hammer—the colors arrested the eye, altering our perceptions of the commonplace.

Kesey and Zane were all smiles as we boarded Further II in our Day-Glo jumpsuits and silly hats. Half of us climbed on the roof, where it was bound to get wild and windy; the other half plopped down in the beanbag den—which had the distinct advantage of being surrounded by speakers so the passengers could groove to manic music and Kesey's Neal Cassady-inspired monologues. Kesey had hijacked the Majic Bus and we were loving every minute of it. Frank, our driver, was in a schizoid state of bus envy and bliss; the Further legend was a part of his fantasy life like nothing else, and now he was playing the role of Kesey copilot in Further II. Captain Kesey, concerned about keeping his crew in sync, had rigged up a microphone system so that two people on the top deck with headphones could report on traffic flows, crowd reactions, police sightings, and other such external factors. Zane and Beth, my assistant, were our top-deck communication links with the subterranean downstairs. Our positions assumed, Further II rolled off into the damp Oregon countryside, with no clear direction, going nowhere slowly, in a blaze of Day-Glo.

Kesey began rapping into the overhead microphone, telling us about the history of Willamette Valley—his equivalent of Faulkner's Yoknapatawpha County. Kesey was raised in this part of Oregon; his brother now runs a creamery in nearby Springfield. Kesey had a yarn to spin about every barn and creek and cow pasture we passed.

But his tone became somber when he told us of Mount Pisgah, a sacred Indian site, where he prayed every Easter Sunday for his son Jed, who died in a freak accident a few years earlier. A van carrying the University of Oregon wrestling team, of whom Jed was a member, had hit an ice patch and slid off a cliff. Kesey was at Jed's hospital bedside when he died. Quoting Faulkner, Kesey once told a reporter: "'Every so often the dog has to battle the bear just so he can call himself a dog again.' I felt the bite of the bear when Jed died. I didn't feel it was God's will that he be up there in a van without seatbelts, without CB to call ahead to a hospital. I felt there was stuff that had happened that was unfair and that could be changed." Wanting to avoid other wrongful deaths, he sued the state of Oregon, the university, and the National Collegiate Athletic Association, won the case, and then turned around and bought the Oregon wrestling team a forty-thousand-dollar van with safety belts and emergency radios. Jed is buried at Kesey's farm next to a chicken coop, not too far away from where the original Furthur rests in peace.

Suddenly, Kesey shifted gears and began talking animatedly about tree farmers and loggers and bears and eagles, free-associating to images he saw in the clouds, just as a light drizzle began to fall. As Further II cruised through the small town of Lowell, we waved to a group of kids on bicycles who howled with laughter on seeing this far-out crew in far-out clothes in the most far-out bus their young minds could imagine. Something about being in this outrageous bus unshackled the mind and soul, and we all screamed with ecstatic delight. Suddenly everything was electrifying, almost holy, in the old Ginsberg-Kerouac way. Holy rock. Holy hill. Holy herd of deer in the holy meadow chewing on the holy grass.

Kesey turned disk jockey, introducing Neil Young's "Sugar Mountain" as "a song that will tell you all you want to know about what it was like in the sixties." Next came Bob Marley's "Redemption Song" and the Grateful Dead's "Truckin'," followed by an old peyote chant by Native American Jim Pepper called "Witchi Tai To." But it was Sam the Sham and the Pharaohs' "Wooly Bully" that really got us going. When I got on the headphones to ask him how the students below were doing, Kesey responded that he had given them "their thee-sis" and "they had all passed with flying colors." As the speakers pounded out loud music, Kesey drove us all over his beloved green corner of Oregon, waving and screaming at every car and person we passed, and finally stopping in front of a rambling farmhouse by a creek, where he parked and ushered us out of the bus.

It was the home of Prankster Ken Babbs, clown prince, instinctive raconteur, idea man, vaudevillian, and longtime Kesey friend. He introduced us to his family and gave us a tour of his home, which included a basketball hoop in the living room and a studio where he mixed audiotapes and acted as archivist of the hundreds of videotapes from various 1960s happenings, including the Merry Pranksters' 1964 bus tour. Babbs led us down to the creek, where we played with his dogs, skipped a few stones, and meandered about. Then it was back on the bus for more outlandish liberation, including a stop in front of a bar where a scene from National Lampoon's *Animal House* was filmed. We returned to the farm—our faces flushed, as happy as pigs in mud—where Kesey put us to work loading hay onto a trailer hitched to the back of a tractor. He took us for a ride to feed his cows, the students tossing the bales off the back to a chorus of hungry moos.

Kesey was truly an incredible host, kind and generous. Back at the house he offered the students beer and soda while pouring himself a stiff bourbon. We then sat around while he played videotapes of the Pranksters with the Grateful Dead (then the Warlocks), Jerry Garcia beardless and innocent looking, a youth rather than a guitar legend. Kesey answered all sorts of questions about the sixties and his life as a writer and warrior.

The students were astounded to learn that he had never seen the movie version of *One Flew Over the Cuckoo's Nest*. He had sold his film rights for only twenty thousand dollars and never received royalties from the movie, but what really galled him was that he felt that Jack Nicholson was miscast in the role of R. P. McMurphy. We talked for a while about *Sometimes a Great Notion*, the story of a family that defies a labor union—and thus their entire community—by continuing to log their forest. The students responded by updating Kesey on what they had learned about the timber wars in Humboldt and Mendocino counties.

Kesey told the students about his third novel, *Sailor Song*, which he had just finished; it's an apocalyptic story that takes place in the early twenty-first century in a little Alaskan fishing village called Kuinak. The lead character, Ike Sallas, is an Earth First!–type eco-radical. (I returned to Oregon that August for Kesey's book party, camping in his backyard for "The Third Decadenal Field Trip." Over a three-day period a thousand people showed up in Kesey's backyard to participate in his Giant Talent Contest, featuring Anne Waldman and bands like Mud Farmers, the Greyhound Daddies, and the Swan and Boogie Patrol Express, all of whom primarily played folk rock. Shoshone poet Ed Edmo performed "Through Coyote's Eyes," and Dead lyricist Robert Hunter read some new poems. Ramblin' Jack Elliot was also there, singing train songs, the blues, and pretty much the whole American songbook. As for *Sailor Song* itself, the novel moved me so much that I decided to bring my students to Alaska for American Odyssey II, for as Kesey wrote: "Alaska is the end, the finale, the Last Ditch of the Pioneer Dream. From Alaska there's no place left to go. . . . So it came down to Alaska, the Final Frontier as far as this sick old ballgame goes. Top of the ninth . . .")

Kesey spoke to the students about comic books and superheroes, with special emphasis on Paul Bunyan, the Lone Ranger, and Captain Marvel. He tossed the I Ching while making frequent references to the Bible, described his 1975 trip to Egypt in search of the occult Hidden Pyramid, and spoke with great respect and fondness about Arthur Miller, Norman Mailer, and Thomas Pynchon. His kindest literary words were directed toward Faulkner and Sherwood Anderson, and he positively lit up when he heard we had visited Jack London's Beauty Ranch. While the students watched another video, Kesey showed me the study where he wrote, and we discussed the state of contemporary literature.

At 9:00 P.M. it was time for the Majic Bus to hit the road. We had spent seven unforgettable hours with Ken Kesey. Before parting, Kesey thrilled the students with magic tricks—coins disappearing in one ear and out the other, playing cards floating in thin air—proving himself a magician through and through. He also handed out calendars of Further II, autographed them, and came outside to tour the Majic Bus. He disapproved of the way the interior was compartmentalized, preferring the open-spaced beanbag living area of Further. He was right, but there wasn't much we could do about our structural arrangements. With handshakes, we said good-bye to our host, moved by his incredible generosity, humor, and humanity. It dawned on me that Ken Kesey was a great teacher because he cared.

Walt Curtis has been called "the unofficial Poet Laureate of Portland." His novella, Mala Noche, *became director Gus Van Sant's first feature-length film. A contributor to early issues of* Spit, *Curtis has published many small-press collections of his work. He is also a well-known artist and an authority on Oregon literature.*

THE WAY IT IS

By Walt Curtis

"If you seek out the spirit,
the spirit will find you."
It's that simple.
If you search for the truth,
you will find the truth.
If you need love
and you are loving—
love will find you.
It's that simple.
This poem is that simple,
but—it's for the next
generation. THIS IS
THE WAY IT IS. THE TRUTH
OF THE UNIVERSE WHETHER
YOU LIKE IT OR NOT.
I like the way it is.

—after talking with Kesey at the
1999 Oregon Book Awards

Mississippi (and University of Pittsburgh) writer Lewis Nordan studied under Kesey's friend John Clellon Holmes (author of the classic Beat Generation novels Go *and* The Horn*) at the University of Arkansas. In late 2001, soon after the publication of his memoir* Boy with Loaded Gun, *Nordan visited classes at Sayre School, a private high school in Lexington, Kentucky, where Jeremy L. C. Jones teaches English.*

✳✳✳✳✳✳✳✳✳✳✳✳✳✳✳✳✳✳✳✳✳

"HERE CAME
A WHITE CADILLAC!"

Lewis Nordan, from an Interview with Jeremy L. C. Jones

Jones: When you were in Arkansas at the university and hanging out with John, did you have any run-ins with Ken Kesey?

Nordan: He came to Arkansas to visit John one time and I was over at John's house and I didn't say much. I just sat in the room in awe of him and he seemed wonderful. I liked him and his wife. They'd had a tragedy in their family at the time. One of their sons was killed in a bus accident from a wrestling party or something like that.

Jones: The school wrestling team . . . the bus went off the side of a mountain, I think.

Nordan: My wife and I had lost a son so I felt a connection with him in that way, and he seemed vigorous and funny and healthy and so on. I kept thinking someday I will be able to be more real and more in the world than I am now, in this depressed narrowed state that I'm in. So I got from him those things. I found him interesting and assertive in conversation in ways that I had not allowed myself ever to be. I felt very much like a Johnny-come-lately or somebody who was a follower rather than a leader, and I admired the way that he was a leader. I liked the way that he and his wife were with each other. I never saw him in his "Wild Man on the Bus" role, but I remember when the twenty-fifth anniversary [edition] of *On the Road* came out there was a big party down in Colorado that all the old beatniks were invited to . . . well, all those who had lived that long . . . So, of course, John went, my friend John Clellon Holmes went. And when he came back, he said all of these people from the early '50s that had known Kerouac, all of them had flown out and were standing around in jackets and ties, sipping martinis, and a cloud of dust arose on the road and here came a white Cadillac convertible with Oregon plates and it was Kesey, drunk and sweaty and sunburned with two cases of beer in the backseat, and they suddenly realized that he was the only one who had *driven* to the *On the Road* party! [Laughter.] The rest of them had become gentrified in the meantime. [More laughter.]

Jones: I only knew him from his work, but I always admired his relentless mischief—his intolerance for things that he felt were wrong . . . and his embracing of things he felt were right.

Nordan: One time I gave a reading out in . . . where was that? . . . Hungry Mind Bookstore? . . . I was thinking it was on the West Coast. Well, anyway, I gave a reading somewhere—maybe it was in Portland. Anyhow, Kesey had read there the week before and they had covered the bookstore. Trash was still on the floor from the Kesey visit. There had been hundreds and hundreds of people there. They had the place filled. When I read the following week, nobody came. I read to like four or five people that worked at the store. That told me where I stood in the literary pantheon. [Even more laughter.]

"Karma (and Other Sermons)" is a talk Kesey gave at the Poetry Project at St. Mark's Church-in-the-Bowery in New York in 1975. It appeared with "Earthshoes" (see p. 138) in The Co-Evolution Quarterly *(Spring 1976).*

KARMA

(and Other Sermons)

By Ken Kesey

Here's a favorite tale of mine from five years ago that, had it a name, might be called "Karma."

It's Christmas Eve, see. We've kept the television off for two weeks. We've got this lady from England named Shirley that's helping us do a traditional Christmas, and it's mellow and warm. Then we hear the dogs barking. I go outside and there's a couple standing in the sleet—one guy you can tell has been in jail because all his features still have that smudgy look like jail tattoos get when they're done with two pens, a matchstick, and India ink—the other a girl looks like if she hasn't been doing speed she should have been doing speed.

They're both dark but they're carrying a blond baby, about eighteen months old, being boldly carried like a lot of children at that time, like a revolutionary poster held up in front of them showing where they stood on things like the nuclear family and soap and water and so forth. I thought, it's Christmas and miserable and no matter how sullen the guy's eyes, or glittering the girl's, I got to invite them in.

At first there was a lot of talk about how wonderful things were getting everywhere as consciousness kept expanding. Then talk about how wonderful it all was, mixed in the same breath with what assholes they had encountered on their journey, how the beautiful far-out people from the holy magical commune they had just left had freaked out and sent them packing for no reason at all, which was for the best anyway because the place was a madhouse and filthy as a pigsty.

The baby had a terrible cough—*nrhack rrrhack rrrhack!* My wife says, "Would you like me to get something for your baby's cough?" The woman says, "No, it's a natural childbirth baby. A triple earth-sign, right? Would you fuck with the healthy balance of a triple earth-sign? I believe doctors are just as unnatural as husbands. The wild animals get by without that kinda crap."

"I believe, I believe"—in her jagged-edge speed voice as bad as any TV hardsell for Tiger Tanks or Hot Wheels. The Dickensian mellowness was fading fast. I got up and began to walk around rubbing my head and knotting my brow and thinking "O Lordy Lordy!" because at this point I knew that these people came either as an answer to a question or as the question that I must have the answer to. Finally the woman got around to changing the baby's diaper, which was mustarded full of a day's diarrhea. My wife says, "Would you like me to get some Kaopectate?" And the woman says, "WHAT THE HELL'S THE MATTER WITH YOU I TOLD YOU IT'S A NATURAL CHILD-BIRTH BABY WHAT ARE YOU TRYING TO DO POISON MY BABY?" The guy hisses, "Shut up you dumb bitch before you get us kicked out!" "YOU SHUT UP, ASSHOLE!" "Bitch!"

And all of a sudden I had to say something that I don't ordinarily say to people unless the condition is desperate or dangerous. But I felt that karma was picking up momentum so fast that my whole living room was in danger of being sucked down with it, so I said, "Look, if you don't stop doing what you're doing here and now, tomorrow and the next place is going to be worse than this, and next week worse than this week, and next year worse than this year, and your next life—if you get another life—worse than this life, until, finally, unless you change your mind, you will just . . . go . . . out."

We, too, have to change our mind and pull out of our karmic nosedive or we are a nation of doomed souls. Here's another sermon I've used, called "Venusians." Outside of Eugene, Oregon, about an hour's drive up into the low logged-over mountains, is the largest piece of untouched wilderness acreage at that elevation in the United States (most wilderness area is really high, above the tree line), untouched by roads or wires. Not so much timberland but the logging industry wanted to get into it tremendously. At first we assumed their lust was for lucre, as usual, then we found that the trees were so big that they were going to have to re-rig the equipment in the sawmills to accommodate trees that size. The deeper we got into it the more we realized that these guys couldn't be wanting to do this for money because it was going to cost more to change the machinery than what they could log.

I thought, it's sexual. Because it's a virgin forest and loggers are loggers there and they're going to get into that forest even if it costs them more than they make. But the more I worked out with them at public hearings and debates, the less I believed this macho motive. Their determination seemed driven, in fact, less by lust than by mechanized mindlessness that is programmed to seek and destroy what is salient and beautiful the way a Holiday Inn will crush a historic home or a rocketing trail bike will home in on the rarest meadow without greed or lust or even the perverse devilish tingle of doing something dumb and evil on fucking purpose and "ya wanta make something of it?" Not greedy, not homey, not even ornery. Just doggedly, blankly, inhumanly determined—as though carrying out posthypnotic orders planted secretly behind those blank eyes by an alien for unhuman reasons.

Non-humans reasons. I began to see them as the victims, not the villains, and when one finally jumped up to screech in overloaded reaction at me, "Listen, mosta you hippies and townies and old ladies and such probably never been up to French Peak and probably never will be!" I found myself completely without anger toward the man. As politely as I could I admitted that it was probably true, just as it was probably true that most of us aren't going to go to the Library of Congress either. But we don't want it logged.

In thirty years when they try to say, "You guys have got it better than ever, living in little cement squares. If it wasn't for this modern technology you couldn't survive." Then we'll need natural places. We'll need to go back and check someplace to see . . . no, no, it's not true: it works, it always works.

There was a force trying to cut out something that was necessary to our survival, to the way that we care for each other. And since I couldn't figure this to be human, I had to assume it was Venusians.

Martin Buber says there's a path of community. It's made up by a nation of people that extends over the whole globe—it knows no boundaries, it knows no ideologies, it knows no policies. It's a nation that has always been in there, in between various conflicting forces, trying to oil the waters as best as possible. It's a nation that knows itself and keeps track of itself, and if you think about it, wherever you've gone you've known this nation and you've always been strengthened by this knowledge.

As exampled when we went to Mexico two or three years ago. Instead of going down to the beach where the Grateful Dead and the cocaine was, my wife insisted we go up into the hills where the Mexicans were. As we walked up the hills—we had to park our car at the bottom—I felt eyes out in the Bougainvillea and saw this seventy-some-year-old woman up there washing dishes. She watched me go back and forth, kept track of me, and if I had come home drunk, had lascivious inclinations towards some of those Mexican girls, got out of line in any way—she would have filled my night with strange arrows. She had that whole number of blocks covered. When we left after three weeks she gave me one nod. It was all I was to get, but it was as strong an acknowledgement of human-to-human as you can get.

Ram Dass explained it this way: he said about four hundred years ago the Baal Shem-Tov, the founder of modern Jewish Chasidism, came to the king and says, "King, the wheat is all poisoned and everybody that eats it this next year is going to go crazy." King says, "That's terrible." And he says, "I thought you would say that, so I have stashed back here enough wheat for you and I to make it through the year and we won't go crazy." The king says, "Now wait a minute. If I'm the king of these people and you're the rabbi to them, ought we not eat the same food and feel the same things so that we have a better idea how to do it?" The Baal Shem-Tov says, "I thought you would say that, too. So I thought that we'd give each other the chance to put a little X on each other's foreheads so that when we see each other later on in the street, we will know that we chose to go crazy, whereas everybody else is just crazy."

And we did. Fourteen or fifteen years ago we chose to go crazy, man, and we know each other. And the only big mistake we ever made was the mistake of thinking for a while that we were going to win.

For a while we began to believe we were going to win. We developed vested interests in the victory to come. We began to parcel off into little groups, it doesn't make any difference which it is. The Krishnas and the Jesus freaks—the literature they're handing out is all battling each other, and yet all of those guys are the same halfway-through-a-step acid-casualty kid who won't go ahead and complete what he started when he lifted his foot up and grabbed the first thing that he came to. One guy grabbed that stick and another guy grabbed this stick, and it set us to fighting each other in all manner and ways.

I drove back across the country last year, from Washington, D.C., through West Virginia. Our country is in terrible shape, folks. One block in any direction off that main Washington, D.C., street is broken glass in the streets. Let me tell you something. That Bottle Bill that we have in Oregon is a good law. If you want to vote for something political, the Bottle Bill is a good one. It provides you with a chance of civilization. Broken glass is against civilization. As long as bottles are coming in and there's no refund on them, they will be broken. If there's a refund on them they won't be. It's as simple as that, and it doesn't cost anybody anything. It's a good law.

Anyway, driving through West Virginia, through this raped country, staying off the freeways where they've landscaped it, through this torn, terrible country, we passed this guy whose face was so much like the country that we didn't really see him out there hitchhiking. We picked him up later on in town when he walked up to the car and says, "Can I get a ride with you guys?" Almost sixty, skinny guy who had done jail time or VA time, wearing khakis, wearing a baseball hat, with a six-pack of beer. I got out the side to let him in the car. Our driver took his hat off, and he's got enormous long hair—it fell way down to here. The guy took a look at him and took a look at me and then rethought his whole situation and started talking, freaked out, and tried to explain his freak-out.

He says: "You guys just don't know. Last year," he says, "a couple young fellers came by here." He says, "I just finished a construction job, I had a lot of money, I had a brand-new suit-case," he says, "these couple young fellers, they pick me up," he says, "they took me outside a town here. Man," he says, "they beat the piss out of me." He says, "I almost got away, up the bank, but one of the suckers got me by the ankles." He says, "I finally got up to the road and I waved a car down and I got into the hospital." He says, "I've been hurt worse than that a lot, by machines and by cars and horses," he says, "but this was different."

And I began to get a sense of what he was talking about, about what women are talking about, about rape. He says, "This was different." And he says, "The cops finally came in about three days and took me back out there to the place and I got out there." And he says, "I saw the grass where it was all bent down and my blood was on it and," he says, "God, they just beat the piss out of me."

And it was like the nation spoke up through this guy. He was saying, some things hurt, deep inside of you. The spirit, the spirit, is hurt in this nation. And all the people whose spirit has not been hurt can help these people.

It doesn't make any difference how much electricity is in those lines or how much gas is in the car out there, if you don't have the spirit, you don't do anything, you don't do jack shit, you lay around. When we begin to think that the spirit comes from something outside of us, we're then conditioned to try to buy it in some way. On the other hand, you can be broke and accomplish a great amount.

BUS STORY #1

George Walker, now a Eugene builder, has recently re-traced the path of the 1964 bus trip in preparation for writing his recollections of that adventure.

DEFINITELY THE BUS

By George Walker

Kesey was often asked what he thought was his most important work. His answer, always the same: "The Bus. Definitely the Bus." Less often asked was how he came to buy the bus.

It all began in November 1963. He had published *One Flew Over the Cuckoo's Nest*, and sold the stage rights to Kirk Douglas. The play was set to open on Broadway that November, and a number of us were in New York for the premier. Ken, family, and friends had all flown out for the event, while I drove alone all the way from Berkeley in my big old Chevy station wagon with a mattress and sleeping bag in the back.

We stayed in New York for about a week, crowding into Carl Lehmann-Haupt's Bowery walk-up apartment, spending our days and nights seeing the sights.

The sights were occasionally enhanced by small doses of peyote, which of course was still legal at that time. The previous summer, Kesey and some of his Perry Lane friends had

cooked down a big mail-ordered-from-Texas batch, boiling it
for days in a huge kettle in his backyard until it was a tar-like
consistency. Double, double, toil and trouble! I carried a 10-oz.
mustard squeeze-bottle of this bitter black goo in my glove box,
along with a box of 1,000 empty triple-0 gelatin capsules.
Squeeze off a couple of those babies, and it would add a bit of
glitter to everything from T-Rex's teeth at the Museum of Natural History to sunrise on the Staten Island Ferry.

Among the day trips we took was a drive out to Flushing
Meadows in Queens, where the New York World's Fair was under construction. It was months before the fair would open, but
with the futuristic architecture apparent in the skinless giant
globe and dome and towers, it was obvious it would be a spec-
tacle. We decided immediately that we would have to come back
the next summer to experience it.

I recalled stories Ken had told of his psychedelic trip the
previous year to the Seattle World's Fair. Ken and Faye, Chuck
and Sue Kesey, and Ken Babbs and his brother John had
gone together, accompanied by some of the experimental chemi-
cals Kesey had appropriated while guinea-pigging for the CIA-
sponsored tests at the VA hospital cuckoo's nest. Kesey's stories
made it sound like great fun, from tripping on the Ferris Wheel
and the Space Needle to stamping fifty-cent aluminum tokens
with slogans for a culture: "Don't Break the Cool," "Don't Bug
the Fuzz," "Don't Carry," and "Stash." I decided immediately
that I wouldn't miss this one. We started talking about returning to New York the following summer.

But of course before we left New York, there was the play.
The afternoon of the great event we gathered at Carl's father's
uptown apartment. As Ken and Faye and the rest of the family—Chuck and Sue, Grandma Smith—were dressing in their
finery for the occasion, a phone call came from yet another
Lehmann-Haupt: Carl's younger brother Sandy. He called to
announce that he had just committed himself to the psych
ward at Bellevue Hospital. A brief conversation revealed that,
since he had committed himself, he could un-commit and walk
out. Luckily we had an extra ticket for the play. Perfect! Seeing

Kesey's vision of the asylum played out on stage ought to show Sandy the folly of a prolonged visit. So Carl and I, and Kesey in his tuxedo, jumped in my Chevy and sped to Bellevue, where we rescued Sandy. Then, back to the apartment to dress Sandy, pack in the rest of our crew, and head off to Broadway and the play. We had spirited Sandy out of one cuckoo's nest into another. Of course we gave him a dose of peyote on the way, and by the final curtain he was converted, if not cured.

When it was time a few days later to return to our homes on the West Coast, Kesey decided not to fly, but to drive back with me. Sandy came along, wanting to see more of these wild people from the west. Kesey and I took turns driving; we slept in the back in shifts. On the second day out, driving across western Pennsylvania, the car radio brought the terrible news: President Kennedy had been shot in Dallas. The news progressed from bad to worse: hospital . . . critical condition . . . confirmed dead. Kesey spoke for all of us: "I don't know who did this, but I know they are the enemy!" We continued driving, and experienced a rare and amazing thing. Everywhere we went, we knew that everybody was thinking about the same thing, in the same way. Ohio. Indiana. Illinois and Iowa. The whole country felt wounded, yet united.

Heading ever west: across Nebraska into Wyoming. We slept out under the stars in eastern Wyoming and woke up under snow. We ate more peyote, bought gold and pink sunglasses, and headed for Jackson Hole, slaloming the car through the blizzard, trying to separate the hallucinated skids from the real slides. Somehow we made it to Lou Breitenbach's ski lodge. That night we rode a toboggan down the mountain in the moonlight, Kesey all the while telling about it to his ever-present portable tape recorder, holding it in one hand while steering the sled with the other.

Another time, Kesey turned abruptly off the highway into the trackless sagebrush to chase a light-struck rabbit. With Kesey, it was always an adventure.

As we made our way west, I thought about the night we went to see *How the West Was Won*. More peyote. It was a premiere showing, in a posh Broadway theater with a guest book in the lobby. Kesey had signed it huge, across a whole page: "Ken Kesey, Captain America." How prophetic, I thought later, when we dressed in flags and red-white-and-blue while driving the bus across America.

It was the following spring when the idea of a bus came to us. Kesey continued to promote the idea of a trip to the World's Fair, and quite a number of his friends were interested. Too many, it turned out, for any one vehicle available. We talked about my station wagon and Ken Babbs' Volkswagen van/pickup, and maybe even a third car to accommodate everyone. Then Kesey and I took a trip to Eugene/Springfield to visit our families, where we found our inspiration. The city of Eugene had quit the transit business. There were no more city buses. Instead, a private company had bought up several small, used school buses, with seating capacities of fifteen to twenty people, painted them emerald green (for the Emerald Empire, as the area is known), and taken over the bus routes. It was a great success; people loved the little buses. They caught our attention, too. If we had one of those little buses, I told Kesey, we could all go to New York in one vehicle. That would be a lot more fun. "Great idea," Kesey said. "Find one and I'll buy it." And so the search was on.

I went to the company running the emerald buses, to see if they had an extra one. No, in fact they wanted more. Clearly they had the local market cornered. I found an old Ford bus on a Eugene used-car lot, and even test-drove it. It was in pretty bad shape. I passed on it. We returned to California, where the search continued. At one point, we considered trying to find a London double-decker bus, and I even advertised for one. Nothing happened. I began reading used-vehicle ads in the newspapers.

During that spring, 1964, Mike Hagen and I had begun experimenting with film and home movies. He was a lot more serious than I was, having bought a nice new 8-millimeter Bell & Howell camera and a film editor. I had my dad's old pre-war Kodak wind-up 8-mm camera, which wouldn't do much. We both managed to edit a few pieces and had a few "shows" at parties at Kesey's in La Honda. We also "experimented" with various psychedelics at some of these gatherings, and soon we were painting things. All kinds of things, from trees to cars to furniture to ourselves, got the many-colors treatment.

One sunny day in May, Faye found the ad I'd been looking for: 1939 International school bus for sale, converted for live-aboard traveling. Complete kitchen, with propane stove and refrigerator, beds sleep eight, dining table, seats, everything we needed. A Catholic family had outgrown it, and was upgrading to a Bluebird. It was in the nearby upscale Atherton neighborhood. We went to see it. It was yellow and huge with big truck tires. Kesey wrote a check on the spot, for $1,500.

We decided Hagen should drive it home, twenty miles over the coastal mountains on the narrow, crooked La Honda Road, as he had driven grain trucks on the family wheat farm in Pendleton. That qualified as experience. He got it to Kesey's without incident. We had a bus. It was long, originally for forty-two passengers, on the biggest chassis International made in 1939, a D50. It was low inside; those passengers were little kids. It weighed almost twelve tons empty, with a giant six-cylinder gas engine and vacuum brakes (barely). Over the next couple of years the 10:00x20 tires, old and worn, would give Cassady a workout, as he eventually changed all of them, one at a time.

A few days after we bought it, we took the bus back over the hill to a junkyard/welding shop in Redwood City, where we started adding to it. Kesey had a hole cut in the roof toward the rear and an old commercial clothes drier welded on to make a sort of turret. Then railings were fashioned out of iron pipe, forward from the turret, to make a riding platform on top. Later, I pried the back window out of an abandoned car to make a windshield for the top. The junkyard provided a steel ladder up the back to the turret, and an extension was welded onto the back of the frame to make another platform, where we would carry a generator, another seat, and my Triumph Tiger 500cc motorcycle, our emergency vehicle. It would provide its own share of emergencies, as various riders would fall off or under it. (Luckily, all injuries were minor.) After a couple of days at the welder, the modifications were complete. We returned to La Honda, and started adding wiring and sound systems. Then it was ready to paint.

By this time, Kesey had decided, at Hagen's urging, to upgrade to 16-mm film. We were going to make a movie of this trip. Hagen and I got a couple of Bolex 16-mm cameras from local pawnshops, along with several old musical instruments that none of us could really play, and Kesey bought twenty rolls of 16-mm color film. We acquired lots of paint and some LSD, and were ready for a painting party. Many friends gathered, and with Kesey's and Roy Sebern's guidance, we painted Furthur. Cassady showed up with tire-changing tools and said he would drive the bus. Zonker rolled a shoebox full of perfect joints.

We were ready for our trip.

Bill Walton, the great UCLA and NBA center, wrote these recollections and reflections at the request of University of Oregon teacher Mark Chilton, whose summer '02 English class was studying Kesey and his work. Walton has been a devoted Oregonian (even though he no longer lives there) since his playing days with the Portland Trail Blazers. A close friend of Kesey's for many years, he is now a television sports analyst and commentator.

THE POINT MAN

By Bill Walton

Great spirits have always encountered violent opposition from mediocre minds.
—*Albert Einstein*

There was nothing quite like bumping into Ken Kesey dancing through the universe when he would graciously alight at yet another Grateful Dead concert. He was the happiest of all the Pranksters. Ken had an endless string of projects, experiments, and ideas that he was constantly working on, incessantly tugging on your elbow. Outside of Moses Malone and Shaquille O'Neal, I don't believe I've ever come across a man who sweated more profusely than this gentle, crazed, and sometimes tormented soul. It is hard to imagine anyone ever having more fun, doing more things, or having more going on in his life than our dear friend and partner, Ken Kesey.

One of my earliest remembrances of Ken was the time we

were all dancing wildly as Jerry lit up the night sky again at Winterland. All of a sudden, from off to the side of the stage, Ken and a small band of his Merry Pranksters paraded right out there onto the stage. A couple of the band members vaguely acknowledged him but mostly everybody just kept right on going about their business. We then realized that Ken was rolling a large cannon out onto the stage. They proceeded to load the massive weapon with the big tamper. They then lit the long, sparkling fuse, setting off a powerful detonation right in the middle of the show. The crowd went absolutely wild; the band played on forever, oblivious to the sideshow.

I was privileged to be part of three of the greatest basketball teams in the history of the game: the UCLA Bruins, the Portland Trail Blazers, and the Boston Celtics. My teammates and friends from those squads have changed and shaped my life. Greg Lee, Maurice Lucas, and Larry Bird were the heart and soul of those great teams. Ken Kesey was the heart and soul of everything that he was ever involved in. He was always the point man in every group dynamic. He made everything he ever touched special. Ken was on the Grateful Dead trip to Egypt in the late '70s, and to see him dominate Cairo, to see him lead the teeming madness of that tour with the Deadheads—even though there were only a couple hundred of them—was to capture the ultimate magic of Ken Kesey.

It made no difference to him what the project, event, or experiment was, Ken only knew life, happiness, joy, and standing on the edge. To see him orchestrate the production of the shows at the Sound and Light Theater at the base of the Pyramids, to see him dominate the hotel, bar, and swimming pool scene at the Mena House, to see him push, command, demand, and drive me to the upper inner chambers of the Pyramids through crawl spaces that even Mickey Hart would have trouble getting through, while I was on crutches and in a cast, was classic Kesey.

Nothing, however, could compare to Ken on the streets of Cairo, in the bazaars, negotiating everything from dinner to the purchase of artifacts, handling the unseemly madness of Cairo's gridlock traffic. Everything in that teeming desert morass ground to a halt because of the millions of cars, jitneys, camels, wagons, donkeys, pedestrians, everyone regularly at the edge of desperation, frustration, and anger. Ken's patience lasted less than a nanosecond in situations like this; he would always pop instantly out of the car—still sweating, always sweating—still crazed and tormented. He became Cairo's chief traffic cop. We didn't realize until later that Ken was not only directing traffic; he was also directing the confluence of divergent civilizations.

You young searchers for truth, justice, and humanity who are enrolled in this course, and have come to love this special man, should know full well that a lot of us have been on this Bus for quite some time. There was the time when Ken, promoting one of his new books, drove the Bus from our beloved state of Oregon down to Las Vegas for the bookseller's convention. A number of us, who were always there whenever Ken needed some extra weirdness, were waiting for him on the northern outskirts of town as this magic Bus rolled in from the great Northwest. The Bus came by and we all got on, once again, and rode this special chariot right down through the Las Vegas Strip— the center of the natural world. The Las Vegas locals and regulars had no idea what to make of us as we cruised up and down the Strip sprinkling magic dust on unsuspecting onlookers.

Now that I have evolved full-time into the world of television, I can safely say that I have never done a television show quite like the one I did with Ken as the host of yet another New Year's Eve special that was fortunately televised throughout the universe that one perfect night in 1987. Ken Kesey, Father Guido Sarducci, and I were the television announcers/commentators for what was certainly a different show than Macy's Thanksgiving Day Parade. When the cavalcade of floats preceding the grand ceremonial entrance of Bill Graham as Father Time rolled in to celebrate the dawn of not just another year but the beginning of a new civilization, Ken Kesey's performance as the live commentator/narrator surpassed anything that Bob Costas, Tom Brokaw, Dan Rather, Peter Jennings, Walter Cronkite, Edward R. Murrow, and Dick Clark have ever done.

During the breaks, we were talking about the incredible transitions that the band was discovering that night. Ken Kesey would never let it go why Larry Bird and Kevin McHale were not participating in this television extravaganza. He was convinced that he had seen them in the crowd that night. He was constantly challenging Larry and Kevin to get up and join us at the broadcast center. If, indeed, Larry and Kevin were there that night, it was probably best for their careers that they didn't participate in this moment of pure bliss, spontaneity, creativity, and madness.

A beautiful thing about Ken is that he was always there, in good times and bad. At Jerry Garcia's funeral, a moment in our lives when words could not express our sadness, loss, and sorrow, Ken, like Maurice Lucas and Larry Bird, was the one who was able to pull us all together, lift us up, and enable us to move forward through the incredible pain, sadness, sense of loss, desperation, and despair that we all experienced. His speech that day allowed us to start the battle anew. Ken Kesey reflected more than anyone the incredible happiness, the incredible joy, the incredible love of life that we all strive for. Ken has also known firsthand the sense of loss and tragedy. The day when his son Jed died in the devastating and tragic car wreck, the day that we all had to go and try to cheer up the man whose only dream in life was to make other people happy—that was as sad a day as any of us has ever witnessed.

Ken Kesey was a man who truly made the world a better place. The simple twists of fate that have changed all of our lives can best be illustrated by the early days of the young Kesey, back in the dawn of this new age—the '60s. Ken was driving this very same Bus (in its earlier incarnation) through the deserts of Mexico looking for yet another spectacular adventure when he saw a young man hitchhiking on the roadside. This teenager, Larry Shurtliff, an Oregon native from the majestic city of Pendleton, was a lost soul who had recently escaped from the oppressive terror of Pendleton law enforcement. Larry was a spirited youngster who did not quite comprehend the scope of "no." He ultimately ran off to Mexico. While Larry was hitchhiking, the Bus came by and he got on.

Ken soon gave him the nickname Ramrod, for his ability to get things done. Ramrod, then a wayward straggler, ascended these very stairs on this very Bus. Who would ever have thought that that would be the career path to becoming the president of the Grateful Dead? That is the kind of power, spirit, and foresight that our leader, Ken Kesey, dispensed on a day-to-day basis throughout his entire life.

As I meditate on Ken's contributions, on his impact, on his ability to change the world, I am sad that I am not able to match his level of commitment to making the world a better place. I have a shrine to Ken in my house, thanking him for being the difference, thanking him for his sacrifices in allowing all of us to freely be who we are. The spirit of Ken Kesey will live forever. The challenge for us is to fulfill his dreams.

Courtesy Lori M. Walton

"The Diverticulum" is the first of four stories by Ken Babbs, scattered throughout this volume, about the celebrated friendship of "the Two Kens." These days, as Cap'n Skypilot, Babbs helps to keep the Prankster spirit aloft on his website, www.skypilotclub.com.

THE DIVERTICULUM

By Ken Babbs

I had too much to dream last night. I'm still all worn out. Kesey hasn't gone anywhere. He keeps jabbing me in the ribs. It's impossible to concentrate. I had way too much to dream last night. We were in some kind of eating place. Wooden, four-sided with the sides angling up to the roof black from the charcoal fire in a long pit in the middle of the floor. The coals were red hot and Kesey slapped a big fish down on the coals. Smoke and steam filled the room. He grabbed a big hunk of metal by the handle and laid it on top of the fish.

The smoke, the smell, the sound were getting to me.

Figures were milling around, wavery, Asians. I was fading fast. I staggered over to a wall to get away from the heat and the smoke. I really had too much to dream last night. I was about to go down and whacked the wall with my fist. The wood gave way and I punched a hole through into the fresh air.

Air, that's what I need. More air. I punched the hole again and made it bigger. The outside of the wall was covered with cedar shakes and they split apart and fell clattering to the ground. Smoke swirled out through the hole and the room started to clear up.

Kesey had on a big glove. He used it to lift the hunk of metal off the fish. The people crowded forward with plates and knives and began cutting up the fish and piling the pieces on their plates.

I had my face near the hole in the wall and was gulping down the air. Kesey came over and held out a plate. I broke off a piece of fish with my fingers and stuffed it in my mouth. All the fires the fish captured glazed my brainpan. Hot geysers shot out my eyes.

"That's a diverticulum," Kesey said, jaws chomping.

I don't get it. Talking's a barrel of furnace slag. Thinking is crows flying in cackling flocks.

"Not the fish. The hole," Kesey says. "It was an ass-saving release. A diverticulum."

I wasn't having any of it. "Give me some more of that fish."

I chewed and swallowed. I definitely had too much to dream last night.

A former rodeo roughstock rider, Paul Zarzyski's recent collections of his poems include "All This Way for the Short Ride," "Blue Collar Light," "Words Growing Wild" (a CD), and "Wolf Tracks on the Welcome Mat." He lives west of Great Falls, Montana.

TWO POEMS

By Paul Zarzyski

Aces & Eights

When I declare my game, when I hammer it
home hard in a poem
that I refuse to deal
life's most glaring imperfection, death,
people, in religious dance-troupe sync,
stepping one giant step
back from the green circular felt,
gaze at me like I'm playing
with a factory-defect deck, like I'm two
tacos shy of the super-combo plate. You bet,
I tell them, Elvis lives. Kesey, I say,
joining Houdini, Garcia, Leary, trust me,
continues to prove further
the universe truly is God's best
magic-trick acid-trip flick
captured in 6-D
on the mother of all real big silver screens. Part illusion,
part hallucination, part very blue

humor—kind of your tie-dyed hybrid cross
between trompe l'oeil and mirage—we,
skipping our own funerals, hating to miss
those hilarious standup eulogy bits, rotate to the
    next table
where, yet again, and don't say I didn't tell you
so, death just isn't in the cards.

Further-Bless-America
Big-Bang Future-Flashback Boogie

> I've enjoyed being a famous writer—
> except that every once in a while
> you have to write something.
> —*Ken Kesey*

On Sunday morning, after the psychedelic
bus rears up out of the Oregon swamp with a High-
Yo-Furthur-'nd-Away into the deepest
cerebral folds of the old cowpoke cosmos,
the woman you love sleeps long past dawn
in her tie-dyed Grateful Dead sweatshirt. Home
last night before the stars even started
to get a buzz on, you escaped the tame,
safe, catered house-warmer, flashed back
past the comfortable, past the contented,
the convenient, the compliant and conformed—past
c-stands-for-average life-style
modifiers, to the Fucking-A-Fulminating,
Fearless, Free-as-in-Woodstock-
Richie-Havens-singing-Freedom, FREEdom!
Forbidden-Fruited '60s. Hungover still
from the Bloody-Maryless '80s and '90s, you scorn

the oxymoron, young republicans,
to end all oxymorons. You'll never forget
your geometrically symbolic youth, the far out
two a.m. television test pattern
you could have marveled at for decades
turning suddenly to static and snow. Now,
craving to relive your sinful magnificence
into the new millennium, you sit squirming,
determined at your November 11th desk,
a flimsy window between you and the aspen
flickering not even the shakiest of its last
few neon leaves, like brain cells, still
barely hanging on
after rocking dusk-to-dawn in a rip-
snorter of a Ken Kesey
launchpad wind. Counting down to Kingdom come's
wildest-ever animal-loving-plant,
plant-loving-animal, electric bash, you lick
not Starbucks but Emiliano Zapata-brand
coffee off your mustached lip
like an aphrodisiac
elixir laced with something illicit
and leftist. Your kaleidoscopic mind
keelhauls all that is not
iconoclastic, climbs aboard the next rocket
bronco out and, following the lodestar
known to us as Poetry, lifts you off,
awestruck, into the eternal
fireworks of words.

Lee Quarnstrom recently retired to southern California after a long career as a journalist, largely with the San Jose Mercury News. "A State of Grace" is excerpted from When I Was a Dynamiter, a memoir in progress.

A STATE OF GRACE

By Lee Quarnstrom

After our April 1965 marijuana bust at Kesey's cabin in La Honda, Kesey found himself established as a true literary outlaw. And while his speaking invitations declined, we discovered that he'd become the darling of liberal Protestants, who were just breaking out the guitars for those "folk-music services" that were becoming popular.

This led to a series of what I could only believe were miracles performed by Kesey. For instance, we were invited down to Asilomar, the Unitarians' Pacific Grove conference grounds at the point where Monterey Bay meets the Pacific Ocean, for the church's annual retreat and whoopdeedoo. Kesey miraculously— or so it seemed—told the enthralled Unitarians one evening to stare out across the ocean. Something big was gonna happen, Kesey predicted, although he admitted he had no idea what it would be. And when the last bit of the sun dipped beneath the horizon, the sky for an instant was painted a neon green, the so-called "green flash," I believe, that people see in Hawaii but never in California.

One day an invitation came from some seminarians studying for the Episcopalian priesthood. Their seminary was in Marin County. Kesey, Babbs, and I drove up that night, so he could speak to the several dozen young students.

Babbs and I sat in the front row, just beneath the stage, in the seminary's combination little theater and forum lecture room. Kesey was on stage, yakking about whatever crossed his mind. He had a carafe full of coffee at his side and a cup on a small table next to him. He asked for questions from the seminarians.

A student up above me toward the back rows asked Kesey, "What about grace? What can you tell us about grace?"

Kesey began to describe athletic grace, the grace of a basketball player, the sort of grace that is often thought of as physical in nature.

I could hear a sad gasp of embarrassment all about me as these seminarians, hoping for some deep religious insight from the burly acidhead author, instead realized that Kesey had misunderstood them completely. They wanted to hear about the grace of God, not the grace of Lew Alcindor.

But they listened politely. And they watched as Kesey poured a cup of coffee and continued to discuss athletes and the graceful way they moved. Then he looked down at Babbs, sitting next to me.

"Hey, Babbs," he asked, "can I have the cream?"

Babbs took the tiny pitcher of cream that was on a small table between us and the stage. He held the tiny cruet by its handle and tossed it through the air. Kesey, still speaking to the seminarians, still describing the grace of an athlete, caught the pitcher by its dainty handle, poured a dollop into his cup and threw it back to Babbs, who also caught it by the handle and replaced it on the little table. Not a drop of cream was spilled during the exchange.

And as he did this, Kesey told the crowd, now silent and awed by this amazing bit of business, that the grace of an athlete and the grace of God are one and the same.

And they suspected that he was right.

"The Alchemists," a linoleum block print by John Lackey

✳✳✳✳✳✳✳✳✳✳✳✳✳✳✳✳✳✳✳✳✳✳✳✳

DEPARTURES:

Three Heavies Take Their Leave

By Ken Kesey

I. Letter to Garcia

Hey, Jerry—what's happening? I caught your funeral. Weird. Big Steve was good. And Grisman. Sweet sounds. But what really stood out—stands out—is the thundering silence, the lack, the absence of that golden Garcia lead line, of that familiar slick lick with the up-twist, at the end, that merry snake twining through the woodpile, flickering in and out of the loosely stacked chords . . . a wriggling mystery, bright and slick as fire . . . suddenly gone.

And the silence left in its wake was—is—positively ear-splitting.

Now they want me to say something about that absence, Jer. Tell some backstage story, share some poignant reminiscence. But I have to tell you, man: I find myself considerably disinclined. I mean, why go against the grain of such an eloquent silence?

I remember standing out in the pearly early dawn after the Muir Beach Acid Test, leaning on the top rail of a driftwood fence with you and Lesh and Babbs, watching the world light up, talking about our glorious futures. The gig had been semi-successful and the air was full of exultant fantasies. Babbs whacks Phil on the back.

"Just like the big time, huh, Phil."

"It is! It is the big time! Why, we could cut a chart-busting record to-fucking-morrow!"

I was even more optimistic. "Hey, we taped tonight's show. We could release a record tomorrow!"

"Yeah right—" (holding up that digitally challenged hand the way you did when you wanted to call attention to the truth or the lack thereof) "—and a year from tomorrow be recording a *Things Go Better with Coke* commercial."

You could be a sharp-tongued popper-of-balloons shithead when you were so inclined, you know. A real bastard. You were the sworn enemy of hot air and commercials, however righteous the cause or lucrative the product. Nobody ever heard you use that microphone as a pulpit. No anti-war rants, no hymns to peace. No odes to the trees and all things organic. No ego-deaths or born-againnesses. No devils denounced, no gurus glorified. No dogmatic howlings that I ever caught wind of. In fact, your steadfast denial of dogma was as close as you ever came to having a creed.

And to the very end, Old Timer, you were true to that creed. No commercials. No trendy spins. No bayings of belief. And if you have any dogma, you surely kept it tied up under the back porch where a smelly old hound belongs.

I guess that's what I mean about a loud silence. Like Michelangelo said about sculpting: The statue exists inside the block of marble. All you have to do is chip away the stone you don't need. You were always chipping away at the superficial.

It was the false notes you didn't play that kept the lead line so golden pure. It was the words you didn't sing. So this is what we are left with, Jerry: this golden silence. It rings on and on without any hint of let-up . . . on and on. And I expect it will still be ringing years from now.

Because you're still not playing falsely. Because you're still not singing *Things Go Better with Coke.*

Ever your friend,
Keez

II. Flowers for Tim

> "Give 'em while they can smell 'em."
> —*Sign in florist shop window*

During the seventies Ken Babbs and I put out a little home-grown periodical called *Spit in the Ocean*. The idea was to have a different editor for each issue and let them call the deal, like in the poker game. Dr. Timothy Leary had agreed to deal our third issue of SPIT from his San Diego prison cell where he was being re-restrained after being recaptured after his escape the year before.

We expected some kind of bleak jailhouse blues, I guess— "Ex-Harvard Prof Gets Down and Dirty Behind Bars!" But no: Dr. Leary writes to inform us that the theme for his issue will be Communication with Higher Intelligence—an ambitious aim even from atop the loftiest ivory tower. But from behind bars?

So Babbs and I fly south to ask our incarcerated editor a few probing questions.

I confess I had some reservations. The famous Dr. Leary had always been more a distant phenomenon than a close friend. Previous attempts at close encounters had always seemed jinxed. The summer of 1961, for example. My family and my Bay Area buddies were booked for a high-level seminar with Leary and Alpert and the International Federation for Internal Freedom down at IFIF's winter paradise in Zihuatanejo. We were bustling our way through the SF airport to our Mexicana flight when we saw the SF *Chronicle* headlines: DOPE DOCTORS ARRESTED AT MEXICO MANSION. Leary, Alpert, and LSD Cronies Given Choice: Go Home or Go to Jail. So much for paradise.

A couple of seasons later we bused our way out to IFIF's digs in upper New York. This northern rendezvous wasn't much more successful than the one that didn't happen down south. Our spirited arrival at the Millbrook mansion was met with a less-than-enthusiastic welcome. Who's to say? It could have been the time wasn't right, or the stars were wrong. Or it could have been the way we came barging up on a sleepy Sunday morn in a gaudy vehicle belching green and orange smoke from beneath the hood and blaring Neal Cassady out the rooftop speakers. Dr. Leary was upstairs, we were informed, sleeping one off. We left before he woke.

So here we were for one more try, in the visitor's tank at the San Diego Federal Pen, waiting for the stonefaced warden to decide whether it's in society's best interest to allow our visit with Prisoner Leary or not. He's taking his own sweet time, too, this warden. He wants to let everybody sit and stew a while. I tip back my chair, pull down my shades, and stew.

I was no stranger to pulling time. But my six-month stretch was at a work camp up in the redwoods. Imagine serving a sentence in this skyless scene, slammed away with Warden Rockface for God knows how long on God knows how many charges! Be a drag. No wonder Dr. Leary let that shadowy gang of revolutionaries called the Weathermen talk him into that swashbuckling escape from the San Luis Obispo slammer last year.

The Weatherman plan? At a quarter to ten Leary excuses himself from the Sunday eve movie in the penitentiary mess hall—nature calls, boss, slips into the kitchen instead of the can . . . ten minutes to ten, up the greasy ventilation shaft above the kitchen range to the roof. Five to ten shinny up the prison's main power pole. If everything went according to plan the Weathermen would blow the transformer out on the street at the stroke of ten. Leary would then have to hand-over-hand along the wire over the wall and down the street-corner pole before auxiliary power cut in. Three minutes. His accomplices would be waiting in the getaway rod.

So imagine: You're a middle-aged psychologist, an alum from West Point, and a discredited prof from Harvard, serving five-to-ten for a fall you took for your daughter at the Texas border when you relieved her of the two stupid joints she had stashed in her panties. Now you're up a power pole on top of a state prison, one eye on your wristwatch while the other contemplates the naked cable that will carry you to freedom, one way or another.

"It was the longest three minutes of my life." Now imagine being spirited out of the country and whisked to Algiers where you are taken in by fellow fugitives Eldridge and Kathleen Cleaver and the Black Panthers who intend to indoctrinate yo pampered ass! Heavy trip or what? Hemmed in by Black Panthers on one side and whitebread weather prognosticators on the other while unscrupulous Algerian cops prowl the street outside the compound, eyes like hungry jackals. Might as well stayed in San Luis Obispo.

Now, picture this: Into this uptight arrangement a sleek and mysterious siren comes swinging to your rescue, sweeps you off your feet then saves you from Black Panthers white Weathermen and jackal-eyed cops alike by marrying you! Seemed like things were looking up at last.

For a honeymoon your new bride wants to take you to her family estate just across the border—meet the folks. But it ain't exactly the folks there to meet you and your bride when the airplane lands. It's four CIA agents, waiting for you with extradition papers and handcuffs. And for your glamorous wife? Handshakes and praise for a job well done. It finally dawns on you: Your mysterious bride is actually bait—hired CIA bait!—and you went for it, hook, line, and glamour.

That's what I really wanted to ask about in that visiting room in San Diego: You're supposed to be this psychedelic wiseman—what wisdoms if any have you gleaned from these ill-fated involvements with beautiful women and borders? What feelings? Did you yearn to kick your daughter's dumb butt? Did you ache to wring your wife's treacherous neck? That's the question I wanted to ask.

Our visiting hour was three-quarters gone when the prisoner was at last escorted in. The guards were polite and the warden was congenial. He even returned Babbs's tape recorder before leaving us alone. The first fifteen minutes on the tape is devoted to *Spit in the Ocean* business. I don't get around to asking my question until the squawk box squawks that visiting is over.

"By the way, Tim, I was wondering . . . what's happening with your new—you know—since you last saw—?"

His recorded response was classic Tim Leary. "With my new spouse the Spy? I see her four, five times a week. She's rented a beach house thirty minutes away by bike. She doesn't have her U.S. drivers' license yet. Sometimes she catches a ride with one of our lawyers."

Babbs and I were dumbstruck. Leary laughed. "I certainly don't hold it against her, her being a spy. She likes this espionage action. It gets her off. It turns her on."

He walked us to the door and waved at the warden behind his bulletproof glass wall.

"Besides," he added, "who am I, of all people, to put down somebody else's turn-on."

And that's my little flower for Tim.

Give 'em while they can smell 'em.

III. Allen, the Friendly Legend

The first time I saw Allen Ginsberg, he was at a party, standing over by the fireplace, and nobody was talking to him. This was after "Howl" but before his big pinnacle. And this woman went over to him and said, "I can't talk to you; you're a legend." And he said, "Yeah, but I'm a friendly legend." He was able to make peace in a way that no one else could, except John Lennon, who had the quality of bringing peace wherever he went. I have three memories of Ginsberg really using these powers.

Back in '66 or '67, we took the bus up to Berkeley for Vietnam Day. The day before the big rally, the Hell's Angels said they were going to protest Vietnam Day by pounding the shit out of the protesters, and they were serious. Since we kind of knew the Angels, we went over to Oakland, to Sonny Barger's house. Ginsberg went with us, right into the lion's mouth with his little cymbals. Ching, ching, ching. And he just kept talking and being his usual absorbing self. Finally they said, "OK, OK. We're not going to beat up the protesters." When he left, one of the Angels, Terry the Tramp, says, "That queer little kike ought to ride a bike." From then on, he had a pass around the Angels. They had let all the other Angels know, "He's a dude worth helping out." They were absolutely impressed by him and his courage.

About fifteen years ago, we had a poetry festival at the University of Oregon, which we held on the basketball court. We invited big names to be the headliners during the evening and auditioned other people during the day. Anyway, as the day went on, people began to drift in. At the end of the day, we had about 3,000 people on the court, and no one had bought a ticket. Ginsberg, he said, "Let me get them." And he took his little harmonium. And he om'd, and pretty soon everybody was going "om, om, om." At the height of the om, he just gestured for the door, and all 3,000 people stood up and walked out so we could charge them five bucks to walk back in through the door. Power.

And the third thing was a time when were driving around. Ginsberg and some others were in the back [of the bus] on a mattress, and we got pulled over by a cop for a taillight or something. The cop looked in the back, and there was Ginsberg on top of this, well, boy, really. And the cop looked in back, said, "What's going on?" "Sir," Allen said, "he is having an epileptic seizure. I have to hold him down." That was it. Phew.

Three examples of his courage and his humor. As all of this stuff comes up, I get all of these images of Ginsberg. I remember there was this picture of him in the newspaper, he'd been at a peace rally, and the cops beat him up. They were carrying him out on a stretcher, all pummeled, and he began flashing the V sign for the reporters taking pictures. Pretty soon, he had everyone laughing, even the cops.

But he wasn't trying to inflame people. There was a time when if you weren't trying to inflame people, you were almost subversive. I can't help but feel privileged to have really known Ginsberg, Timothy Leary, and Jerry Garcia. Those are three heavies, and as time goes by and all this hysteria about drugs wears off, these guys will be re-evaluated in terms of their work and their effect on society. All three were real revolutionary leaders—like Benjamin Franklin or Jefferson—and it's the same revolution, the revolution of consciousness, without which the nation will not survive. We've got to be mature enough to incorporate everyone into this revolution. Its basis is mercy and justice, and mercy before justice.

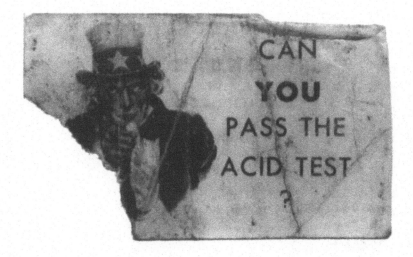

The novelist, essayist, and poet Wendell Berry was in the Stanford University writing program with Kesey and Babbs in 1958–59. He wrote "Kentucky River Junction" after Ed McClanahan took Kesey, Babbs, and several other Pranksters to visit him at his Henry County, Kentucky, farm in 1970. The poem appeared in Apple #5, 1971.

KENTUCKY RIVER JUNCTION:

A Letter and a Poem

By Wendell Berry

April 18, 1970

Dear Ed,

I thought at first that this poem was going to include the whole party of you. But finally it seems to have come out of my sense of where Kesey and Babbs and I have got to, having started out together in that writing class at Stanford in the fall of 1958. That class failed to be any kind of meeting ground. My own contribution to its failure was a scared conviction that life was a contest and that I, having wandered out of my league, was about to get done in. And so I came on all year like Captain Critic, sure that everybody there was the sworn enemy of Henry County poets. Which is a wonderfully efficient way to avoid making any friends. I don't, of course, know what was on anybody else's mind, but the failure I sensed in that class may have been my own entirely.

I think the crisis of my life was the discovery that I was a Henry County poet, a kind of creature that, so far as I knew, had no precedent in creation, and that I feared was contrary to evolutionary law. I think I went around for years suspicioning that I was the sole member of an otherwise non-existent species. It was like I began with one foot on the ground, very uncertainly balanced, and all my work has been the slow descent of the other foot. Now I think the other foot has come all the way down and planted itself in Henry County along with its mate. And that was the only way I could get my head free of the fear and the combativeness I used to feel. I mean when a Henry County poet begins at last to see himself as one of the natural possibilities of Henry County, and not as an evolutionary accident, then he quits worrying so much about getting stomped out, and begins going around, grinning, saying over and over to himself: "I am possible. I am possible." And having become convinced of the possibility of so odd a creature as himself, he joyfully concedes the possibility of a Kesey and a Babbs—and a McClanahan and a Norman and a Hall, and rare creatures of all sorts. And that's a long way from my old wish that people would confirm my existence by agreeing with my opinions.

Now about this poem. I wrote it right after you all were here, and have kept it around ever since, trying to see if I thought it would mean anything to anybody but me. I can't tell. If you think it's any good, show it to Kesey and Babbs. But show it to Gurney and Bill Root first. If you don't think it's any good, throw it away. What I want is to make those men a good gift, and I can't think of any worse gift than a bad poem.

We're horrendous busy here, and getting busier. Saving the World, and all that. I'm going to try to quit this public shit before long and get sane.

Love to Kitty, the kids, et al
Wendell

Kentucky River Junction

To Ken Kesey & Ken Babbs

Clumsy at first, fitting together
the years we have been apart,
and the ways.

But as the night
passed and the day came, the first
fine morning of April,

it came clear:
the world, that has tried us
and showed us its joy,

was our bond when we said
nothing.
And we allowed it to be

with us, the new green
shining.

　　　*

Our lives, half gone,
stay full of laughter.

Free hearted men
have the world for words.

Though we have been
apart, we have been together.

　　　*

Trying to sleep, I cannot
take my mind away.
The bright day

shines in my head
like a coin
on the bed of a stream.

*

You left
your welcome.

BUS STORY #2

Chloe Scott, a dancer, dance teacher, and professional practitioner of the Feldenkrais method of physical therapy, still lives in the Perry Lane neighborhood. She is writing her memoirs

✳✳✳✳✳✳✳✳✳✳✳✳✳✳✳✳✳✳✳✳✳✳

NO FURTHUR

By Chloe Scott

I was never a Prankster, Merry or otherwise. Pranksterism sprung up around me like a rank untidy growth when we all lived on Perry Lane in the late fifties, early sixties. I moved to one of the small cottages built there after the First World War, with my seven-year-old daughter, Jennifer, after divorcing my husband and leaving New York forever. A one-block street, its official name was actually Perry Avenue, but no one ever called it that. The little houses were surrounded by greenery, and an oak tree grew in the middle of the street.

Perry Lane, pre-Kesey, was even then an enclave of independent thinkers and intellectuals. I lived next door to one Robin White, a published novelist, who was, as was I, ten years older than the grab-bag collection of Stanford grad students clustered around in the other cottages. Robin lived there with his wife and three children and their house was open to everyone. He saw himself as the focus of social action on the Lane. The flavor of this free-spirited collection was old-time Bohemian with a tang of West Coast laissez-faire. Partying was frequent, low-key, and alcohol-based. Candles burned and dripped in the necks of wine bottles, everyone wore sandals, and some of the guys grew beards.

When Kesey bombed onto the lane in 1958, the atmosphere changed both gradually and radically. He arrived one day with Faye, his high-school-sweetheart wife, and moved in next door to me. . . . His first words on meeting me were, "Hi. You look like Lizzie Borden"—said with a smirk and a slight chuckle.

This did not endear him to me. In fact I never did understand what made him say it. (The rhyme he referred to goes: "Lizzie Borden took an axe,/Gave her mother forty whacks,/And as soon as she was done,/Gave her father forty-one"—an actual murder case in the nineteenth century.) Hardly a flattering reference, especially since Lizzie Borden was reputed to be a dried-up old maid. And here I was, the queen of Perry Lane. Unfortunately, it was typical of a kind of humor Ken favored.

Ken was at Stanford as part of what was to become one of the most famous and successful classes in the history of Wallace Stegner's creative writing program. Writers from the class began gathering at one or another of the cottages for regular, serious literary meetings and readings, Larry McMurtry, Peter Beagle, and Gurney Norman among them. And the flavor of the parties changed. Two of the grad students introduced weed, still in those days a novelty. Smoking dope was exotic, and at first only one's musician friends did it, but soon everyone did. And the Bohemians morphed from bebop to hipster to cool to Beat. Perry Lane echoed to the rapping and banging of bongos, day and night. It was an eternal party. How did we have so much time? I was working, teaching dance. Presumably the students were studying, the writers writing, but my recollection is of one long party, and it never rained. Ken brought us psychedelics from the VA Hospital where he worked while he wrote *One Flew Over the Cuckoo's Nest*, and again the intensity of the partying escalated.

But the partying, the dope, the crowds of strangers attracted to our little settlement began to be unpleasant, too much of a good thing. . . . After one weekend away, I returned to my cottage to find four totally unknown trespassers sleeping there. Enough, I said. Jenny was twelve years old at this point, and was being exposed to what I saw as unwholesome influences. Before the outsiders overran us, the carryings-on had been more in the nature of hijinks and fun and games. But now the cops were nosing around, neighbors were complaining, there was an ominous sense of things being out of control.

And then with the suddenness of an avalanche it was over. The property on which all the houses stood was sold. Everyone was evicted. At a final monster farewell block party, Ken led an attack on an old upright piano, demolishing it with an axe, and amidst the twanging and sproinging of springs in their death throes, set it on fire. Then everyone was dispersed to the four winds. Which was when the Keseys moved to La Honda and another chapter began, in which we saw the birth of Hippiedom.

Their rustic house, set on the edge of a redwood forest park by the side of a stream, was reached by crossing a narrow, rickety wooden bridge, just wide enough for an automobile. "The scene" had moved with them, over the hill, and the spread was quickly thronged with ex–Perry Laners and other flavors of friends, fellow-travelers, hangers-on, freeloaders and dopers of many stripes. Amongst them were a few serious artists of the caliber of Joe Lysowski, painting psychedelic fantasies, and Ron Boise, who clanged away under the trees, creating his larger-than-life metal sculptures. Many of these folks stayed in the Kesey cottage, while others camped around in tents and trailers or went home to their lairs at night.

Somewhere along in this time, 1963 to 1964, the Great Cross-Continental Bus Trip notion was born. The plan for the big trip began evolving on a drive George Walker and Ken took after the opening of *Cuckoo's Nest* in New York. On their drive home to Oregon they came up with the idea of taking a group of friends from the West Coast and driving to the projected World's Fair in New York the next year, recording the trip on

16-millimeter film and audiotape, to include pranking around at the fair itself and then the return journey. What a gas. What a novelty. What fun. The only problem: how to transport all the folks who were sure to want to be included. After various possible solutions (a fleet of station wagons, VW buses) were discarded, the brilliant notion of a school bus occurred to someone. A retired school bus was acquired, one that had already been modified into a sort of camper with built-in bunks and refrigerator and sink. The Pranksters set upon it and modified it even further. A rack was affixed to the roof for people and equipment, with a ladder to the top. A sound system was installed. And day by day, the exterior was transformed by the streaks, stripes, strokes, and swashes of paint: Day-Glo, nightlight, rainbows of swirling color overlaid and overlapped on its capacious yellow sides.

It was somewhere along about this time that the Merry Pranksters got their name, and their mission, as Intrepid Travelers, was clarified: Pranksters were Till Eulenspiegle on acid. Thumb your nose at authority. Show up the absurdities of modern life. Prick the pride-balloon of the squares and the uncool. But not just to make them look stupid. Leave disruption and confusion in your wake but also possible delight and amusement. Give them a fresh look at things, open up possibilities for liberation and enlightenment. Ken, the Chief, as Swashbuckler and Ken Babbs, his second in command, as Intrepid Traveler, along with Neal Cassady as Sir Speed Limit, would lead these bold pilgrims on their quest. . . .

The bus is ready. The first, the original, the prototype of a painted-up hippie bus stands before us with its glowing chaos of color, its sign on the front, FURTHUR, and one in the back saying CAUTION: WEIRD LOAD. A motley crowd is gathered in the sun, gaping, admiring. Climbing on and off, checking this and that, the pioneer crew load baggage and stake claims on the space inside. Sleeping bags, backpacks, duffel bags, old suitcases, paper bags, plastic bags, any receptacle that could be stuffed with belongings is piled aboard and quickly swallowed up in the total chaos. Equipment—electrical cords, connections, plugs, cables, mikes, batteries, film, tapes—is collected and stowed inside and on top of the bus in untidy piles. Speakers blare Beatles. Ken oversees it all, trekking back and forth across the dusty sward in his old sneakers, checking the progress of the packing and provisioning, carrying boxes and bags and belongings.

At last, after weeks of preparation, they are set to go. I stand with the other non-tripsters, saying goodbye and bon voyage. The adventurers climb aboard, spreading themselves around on the benches and seats, hanging out the windows.

"Keep in touch!" we call to each other. "Don't forget to write!"

Cassady takes the wheel, bobbing and bowing to the ones left behind, now standing forlornly in the dust. The engine growls to life and throbs steadily. With a grinding of gears and a slight lurch, the bus inches forward, moving toward the bridge. The crowd cheers. Everyone is waving. Slowly, Cassady maneuvers the ponderous bus onto the creaking planks, rolls forward a few feet, then . . .

With a cough and a splutter, the engine dies. The bus stops.

Repeated noise of engine being turned over, *eheheheheh*. Nothing.

Again: *eheheheheh*. Nothing.

Someone turns off the music. Everyone looks at one another.

A shout from the driver,

"OUT OF GAS!"

in the middle of the bridge, and that was the beginning, and a perfect metaphor for the whole bus trip.

WALKING WITH THE KING

By Hunter S. Thompson

Nearly forty years ago. That's incredible. It seems like at the most forty months. It was a wild time, folks—the good old days for sure. We stomped on the terra. San Francisco in 1965 was the best place in the world to be. Anything was possible. The crazies were seizing the reins, craziness hummed in the air, and the heavyweight king of the crazies was a rustic boy from La Honda named Ken Kesey.

He had the craziest gang in the West. LSD-25 was legal in those days, and Kesey's people were seriously whooping it up. It was a whole new world. "Do it now" was the motto, and anything not naked was wrong. The best minds of our generation somehow converged on La Honda, and Kesey had room for them all. His hillside ranch in the canyon became the world capital of madness. There were no rules, fear was unknown, and sleep was out of the question.

How I became involved with these people is a long, queer story. I'd done an article on the Hell's Angels for *The Nation*, and once that was out I had my entree. After that, as far as the Angels were concerned, I was "good people." As for Kesey, I always liked his work and believed then, as I still do, that he was one of the really good writers of our time. Earlier, I'd been to one of the Prankster things at Kesey's La Honda place and I liked it.

I happened to have a foot in both camps, and what I did basically was act as a social director mixing a little Hell's Angel with a little Prankster to see what you came up with—for fun, of course, but I was also acting in my own interest because I wanted to have something interesting to write about. To do this safely, well, you must have control. My control ran out early on.

To the credit of Kesey and the Pranksters, they were too crazy to be scared. Kesey invited the boys down to La Honda for a full-scale set-to with scores of Angels converging for rapine, LSD, and fried chicken. I told Kesey that he would deserve to be shot as a war criminal if he went through with this. I remember thinking, "What the fuck have I wrought out here? I have destroyed all kinds of things I've been entrusted to at least be careful with." I was opposed but there wasn't time to be opposed, there was only time to turn on my tape recorder.

I remember the hordes snarling down the road and amassing near the big welcome banner the Pranksters had stretched across the gate. At the entrance stood the young innocents eager to extend their tribal hospitality.

It was quite a scene. People were bursting into flame everywhere you looked. There were speakers all around in the trees and other big delay speakers on the cliff across the road, with wires. And there were about six cop cars parked in the road, flashing lights, cops everywhere, they could see right across the creek. And all the while more Angels were coming down the road and being welcomed with great happiness and friendliness. The simple fact that carnage was averted was impressive, but this was incredible.

Yep. That was Uncle Ken. He couldn't laugh unless he was going fast, and then you couldn't hear him at all because the wind made his lips flap like rubber.

One thing he never knew, though, was what it felt like to get from his house back to mine in thirty-three minutes on a 650BSA Lightning. It was fifty-five miles: which is very, very fast. But there was no speed limit on Highway 1 back then: and on most nights there was no traffic. All you had to do was screw it all the way over and hang on. Everything after that was like being shot through the looking glass. It was faster than a brain full of DMT—one of the most powerful psychedelics ever made. As Grace Slick observed one day, "Acid is like being sucked up a tube, but DMT is like being shot out of a cannon."

Maybe I have gone faster, since then, but somehow it's always felt slow.

———————

Uncle Ken and I often corresponded for no other reason but to stay in touch. Here is one from Mobile Bay back when Ronald Reagan was in the White House and the so-called war on drugs had good people paranoid:

December 12, '81

Dear Ken,

If you thought the air was bad in China, you should smell Mobile in the rain at four-thirty on a cold Saturday morning. I just got back from the Waffle House across the bay, where I spent about two hours eating steakburgers and reading your Beijing piece in Running and drinking a hell of a lot of coffee, because a man with no hair and short pants can't just hang around a Waffle House on the edge of Mobile Bay at four o'clock in the morning without running up a tab, especially when he's laughing a lot and ducking outside in the rain every once in a while to hunker down in a big red Cadillac car for a drink of good whiskey and a few whacks of rotten cocaine.

Risky business, all in all. You want to get down under the dashboard for that kind of action, and lock the electric doors. The parking lot of a Waffle House on Interstate 10 is a bad place to get weird, and it's even worse if you keep coming back inside and reading the same goddamn magazine and make the waitress jumpy by laughing out loud every few minutes and smacking the orange countertop and smoking Dunhill cigarettes in a holder.

Jesus Christ, that was a hell of a long article. I kept thinking I could finish it off with maybe just one more whack of Wild Turkey and two more quick snorts—but the fucker kept on going, like a thing I might have written myself, and when I finally finished the bastard I tipped that fishhead bitch five dollars and drove like a bastard across the bridge, eight miles in five minutes.

It was the most fun I've had in a while, and a really fine piece of writing. I'm going to have a word with Perry about the unfortunate slip into damaging personal libel, with regard to my own persona and future earning power, but I figure that's something we can settle out of court. An ounce should cover it, I think.

Anyway, it's good to see that you're finally beginning to learn something from the fine example I've been trying to provide, for lo these many years. And never mind those jack-offs who keep saying you'll never make it as a sportswriter. Fuck those people. You just keep at it, Ken, and someday you'll be like me.

Okay, see you next time I get up into Rape Country, and meanwhile, write just a little more often. I could use a few more good nights in the Waffle House. That was fun, man. If the piece had gone on for a few more pages, I'd have ripped the apron off that fishhead woman and fucked her right there on the stove.

Hello to Babbs and the family. And tell Perry that I'm into serious training for London. By the time I get through with those dilettante limey bastards, they'll wish they were back in Dunkirk.

But until then, you've set a new standard, and it gives me real pleasure to salute it.

Your friend,
Hunter

Glen Love is a professor emeritus of English at the University of Oregon. "The Words on the Page" appeared (under a different title) in the Eugene Register-Guard shortly after Kesey's death

✳✳✳✳✳✳✳✳✳✳✳✳✳✳✳✳✳✳✳✳✳✳✳

THE WORDS ON THE PAGE

By Glen Love

Nov. 16, 2001

As a teacher of American literature at the University of Oregon for many years, with a special interest in Northwest literature, I always looked forward to teaching Ken Kesey's novel, *Sometimes a Great Notion*. I could tell students, of course, of the importance of place in literature. I could tell them of the characteristic American obsession with building one's own world, with shaping one's outer reality, one's house, for example, to conform to a private inner vision to be shared, if at all, with only a chosen few. I could point out how this American sense of creating one's own world-as-house differs from the attitudes more common in older countries and cultures, where individuals are expected to fit their lives into patterns that have stood for centuries, and whose structures of living are already formed and waiting for them—the sorts of structures that English writer Virginia Woolf rebelled against in *A Room of One's Own*.

I could go on to explain the primacy of the house as a controlling idea in much classic American literature: Natty Bumppo and Mohegan John's forest hut in Cooper's Leatherstocking novels, Thoreau's spare, scrubbed little cabin at Walden Pond,

Huck Finn and Jim's raft home on the great river, the wandering Joads of Steinbeck's *The Grapes of Wrath*, scattered and dispossessed, their tragic vulnerability made clear by what critic John Milton called their houselessness.

The examples may be carried out endlessly. The subject is one of the givens in American literature. But I could never be quite sure that students got it, until they began reading a locally set novel like Kesey's *Sometimes a Great Notion*. Then, I'm fairly sure they know. They know in that fine way of knowing which comes only when an idea intersects with one's own personal experience. They know because they've seen the Stamper house, or one like it, across the Siuslaw River from the highway to the coast, between Mapleton and Florence. Or perhaps on a bend of the Umpqua above Scottsburg on the road to Reedsport.

They've seen such a house, above "a river, flat as a street, cement-gray with a texture of rain . . . an ancient two-story wood-frame house [that] rests on a structure of tangled steel, of wood and earth and sacks of sand like a two-story bird with split-shake feathers, sitting fierce in its tangled nest."

They know how the "rain drifts about the windows," how rain filters through a haze of yellow smoke, and how "the sky

runs gray, the smoke wet yellow. Behind the house, up in the shaggy hem of mountainside, these colors mix in windy distance, making the hillside itself run a muddy green."

Once they've finished reading Kesey's description of this fierce house, shored up against the relentless pull of the river with logs and cables and burlap bags filled with rocks and cement and wire rope and cables and logging chains, there can be no question in their minds about the American house as a fit container for that which it contains, a metaphorical expression of its dominant inner life. Here is a striking objectification of the toughness and mettle of the Stamper males. A race of dinosaurs, perhaps, but the subjects of an unforgettable portrait of Oregon life, whose motto will be, as the house proclaims, and as the crudely lettered plaque on Hank Stamper's wall shouts, "Never Give A Inch!"

Ken Kesey, like Hank Stamper, came by his toughness honestly, and it fit beautifully with a long and effective tradition in American fiction: the sensitive roughneck, it has been called. The tough guy with soul. Herman Melville got his training in the school of hard knocks, aboard a whaling ship, which he termed sardonically, "my Yale College and my Harvard." Walt Whitman adopted a persona, not as Walter but as "Walt," "one of the roughs. . . . Washes and razors for foo-foos, For me, freckles and a bristling beard." Stephen Crane played baseball for Syracuse University, and gravitated toward the slums of New York for his apprenticeship as a reporter and writer. Jack London grew up tough and in poverty among the waterside docks of Oakland. Ernest Hemingway played high school football (not very well), skipped college, rushed off to war, and was always proud of his skills as a boxer, hunter, and fisherman. Ken Kesey won a wrestling scholarship to the University of Oregon, and partied with the Hell's Angels, who "took to Kesey right away . . . a stud who was just as tough as they were," as Tom Wolfe put it.

Kesey's fictional heroes are tough guys, but, like Kesey himself, there is something important under the bravado. Harding in *One Flew Over the Cuckoo's Nest* and Lee Stamper in *Some-*

times a Great Notion are versions of the intellectual, and Kesey was something of an intellectual, too, or he could never have written so well. But he was smart enough to keep it hidden under a public personality which launched him into fame. He was artful, but it was the art of grit, as my friend Gil Porter calls it in his book on Kesey by that title.

F. Scott Fitzgerald once claimed that there were no second acts in American lives. I think he referred to the fate of our celebrities, what happens to our film stars, our champion athletes, our artists, who often hit it big early, blaze into fame and notoriety, then often just as quickly burn out and are forgotten. One thing I admire about Ken Kesey is that he continued to live and work and be himself beyond the dazzle of his two great early books, beyond the hyperesthesia of the 1960s, beyond the cultism and media fame that surrounded him, and that he perhaps courted and enjoyed.

I think of him continuing to write, not only memorable works like *Sailor Song* and *Last Go Round,* but letters to *The Register-Guard* about field-burning smoke, back in the days when we used to choke on it regularly, and careless speeders through Kesey's home town of Pleasant Hill, and the need for teaching high school kids the classics instead of pop lit. "Teach *Moby Dick,*" he told local high school English teachers. "We'll take care of the psychodrama here at home."

I think of Kesey giving thirteen grad students in writing at the University of Oregon a tale they can spin to their grandchildren, in composing and publishing a collectively written novel, *Caverns* by O.U. Levon (who turns out to be U.O. Novel spelled backward). I think of Kesey putting on a suit and tie and sitting still like a good Rotarian long enough to receive the University's Distinguished Citizen Award at a graduation ceremony some years ago. I think of Ken and Faye Kesey enduring the anguish of losing their son in a highway accident, a student here at the University of Oregon and on the wrestling team. I think of the parents honoring their son with the memorial atop Mt. Pisgah. I think of Kesey keeping his name in the phone book all this time, and all the youngsters who had heard of him and wanted to see or speak to a legend, all the aging flower children, still crazy after all these years, hoping to tap in once again to The Source. There he was, in the phone book.

Ken Kesey showed us how to live when the hype is over and the tumult and the shouting dies, and life returns, as it does, to just muddling through.

Of course, muddling through, for Kesey, would still, for the rest of us, resemble something closer to a roller-coaster ride. For he was always a shade bigger than reality, and we sensed it, and wanted to be around him.

Sole, incomparable, the Hulk Hogan of our literature.

But after all it is his two great novels that will shoulder him into the Hall of the Immortals. The words on the page. Language, stories, images that live and give meaning to our lives and the place where we live our lives. Language which, to cite Robert Frost, reminds us of what we didn't know we knew. Kesey's work, especially *Notion*, joins a handful of books, like Frances Fuller Victor's *River of the West*, H. L. Davis's *Honey in the Horn*, and Don Berry's *Trask*, which define the Oregon country. So, while we celebrate the joy and spirit of his life, we can look forward to returning to his books, to the words on the page, for those pleasures that time does not diminish.

THE TOOTH

By Ken Babbs

If I were asked to pick one word to describe our relationship, a good one to use would be toothsome. We were a toothsome twosome.

When we were at Stanford he got me to work out with him in the wrestling room. I was no match for him since he had wrestled in high school and college, but I was live meat he could throw around and he taught me a few basic moves.

Then he signed me up for the intramural wrestling tournament. He couldn't participate because he was a college letterman. It was the 198-pound division and he figured I could win if I got past the redheaded muscle man in the gym who had obviously done a lot of wrestling. As luck would have it I drew the redhead as my first opponent.

Luck of the draw. I was also playing intramural basketball and had a game the same day as the wrestling match. The game was over at five and I was scheduled to wrestle in a half hour. I was already bushed.

"It's okay," he said. "I've got just the boost."

He handed me a little white pill, a cross-top. I popped it and he took one, too—"to be on the same vibe."

"With this guy you've got to get him right away," he said. "Otherwise he'll get ahead on points and ride you all night. Go for the quick takedown and pin."

We decided on the old dive for the ankles, yank him off his feet and leap spreadeagled across his chest trick.

Everything went as planned. I dived for the ankles and yanked and he went down all right, but not backwards. He fell forward and drove my face into the mat; flipped me over while I was still dazed and pinned me in three seconds flat.

Not till I staggered off the mat did I realize I'd broken a front tooth. By next morning my tongue was shredded, worrying the jagged edge all night on the jagged edge of the cross-top. We listened to dolorous music on the hi-fi until morning and then he drove me to the dentist.

Over the years I've lost that front tooth a time or two but always at home so I was able to get it replaced. He wasn't so lucky.

When he was on the run from the law, he was driving through Oakland with his lawyer yakking strategy when the car in front slammed on its brakes. He plowed into its rear, smacked his face on the steering wheel, and came up groggy.

"Beat it," his lawyer said. "I'll handle this."

He scooted, leaving his front tooth behind.

The mad dentist in Santa Cruz made him his famous flag tooth: a blue star with alternating red and green stripes. It served him well for a year or two—until the day he was feeding the ducks and let fly a tremendous sneeze. A duck snagged his tooth before it hit the ground. He penned up the birds but after two days of pawing through duck droppings he gave up.

It was the end of an era. No more toothy camera poses for demanding photographers. No more showing off to visitors come to see his famous tooth. A normal smile was a relief.

Until we drove to San Francisco on one of our numerous Bay Area missions of enlightenment and he lost his tooth again. Chinese food did him in. Litchi nuts. The tooth nestled pearly white amongst sweet-and-sour pork.

On the ride home we stopped at a convenience store and he sprawled across the seat. Hagen held the flashlight. M.G. pried open his mouth. I put a dollop of super glue on the tooth, positioned it and jammed it home.

When we got back the dentist fixed it for real, saying don't ever put super glue in your mouth. It destroys whatever it touches.

What did he know? Flash-forward to the Rock and Roll Hall of Fame tour. The bus traveled to Chicago on a flatbed trailer. The rest of us followed by air. This time the in-flight package of treats was the culprit.

"Triage, triage," he yelled, when we rendezvoused with the bus. Everything had to be taken out, spread on the ground, and reassembled. He lay on the floor of the empty bus, head propped back, flashlight illuminating the crater where his tooth once lodged. It was a tricky move, requiring a half twist to get the superglued tooth onto the stump, but it held.

Until we were on the road, headed to Cleveland and the Rock and Roll Hall of Fame. The tooth or the glue or the dirty fingers had caused an infection and his lip and cheek were grotesquely swollen. He looked like a punch-drunk fighter. The tooth was wrapped in a napkin and stuck in his pocket.

We pulled into Ann Arbor to go to Borders Books: regale the fans with bus lore and pranksterdom; sign books and posters. We meandered through an office park and pulled up in front of a building. He was pawing through CDs getting ready for the grand entrance at Borders, not aware we weren't anywhere near the bookstore. His nephew Kit was driving. Kit turned in his seat and waited. Mother Superior, the Rock and Roll Hall of Fame organizer, stepped forward.

"We're at the dentist's," she said. "I called ahead. You can get that tooth fixed and some antibiotics for the infection."

He looked up. "We don't have time for this nonsense. We've got a job to do. Take us to Borders, Kit."

Kit laughed and held out his hand. Mother Superior dug in her purse and coughed up a five-dollar bill. Kit had bet her his uncle would never go through with her plan.

She did get some antibiotics somewhere and that killed the infection, and after we got home he went to the dentist for a replacement and another lecture.

The tooth stayed put until just before he was scheduled to go into the hospital for his operation. It popped out while he was home gnawing a barbecue rib. He had it put back in but it didn't feel right. He didn't have time to go back to the dentist. He went to the hospital instead. After his operation, while he was in recovery, it fell out again.

I was visiting him and he had me go in the closet and find his shaving kit. There was a tube of super glue in it he kept for emergencies. He lay back on the hospital bed and I superglued the tooth back in. He felt a lot better, once again flashing a big smile.

A couple days later his smile was gone. "What happened to your tooth?" I asked him. He grimaced. "That super glue never did work all that well."

"You want me to try again?"

"It's gone. "

Gone? Yep. It had come out when he was eating and he set it on the tray and fell asleep, and when he woke up the tray was gone and so was his tooth.

He never did get it back. The last time I saw him he was lying in his casket, eyes closed, hands crossed. He looked good, dressed in his western garb, except there was something wrong with his face. His mouth was gripped tight, in a grimace. To cover the missing tooth, I realized. Damn. I wish he hadn't lost that tooth. Without it he wouldn't smile and he had a great smile . . . a wonderful smile.

Pat Monaghan, a native Kentuckian, taught high school drama and English in Sacramento for many years. His seminal high school stage production of Cuckoo's Nest *in 1969 begat the successful Little Fox Theater production in San Francisco, which in turn begat the 1973 New York revival and, eventually, the Michael Douglas film (which Kesey resolutely refused to watch). Monaghan is now retired, and lives in Santa Cruz.*

THE CHARACTER

McMurphy Goes to High School

... and Gets an A!

By Pat Monaghan

It was a dreary day in mid-November of 2001 in Santa Cruz, California, when I checked my e-mail and noticed a posting from my old friend Ed McClanahan, describing his visit to Oregon and the death and funeral of his friend Ken Kesey.

I had last heard from Ed back in May, when he brought to my attention an article from the Arts section of *The New York Times* about Kesey's having gone to New York to see the most recent revival of the play based on his novel *One Flew Over the Cuckoo's Nest*. The article further described Kesey's backstage visit to congratulate the lead, Gary Sinise, on his performance. In doing so he told Sinise that his favorite production of the play had been done many years before (more than thirty, in fact) by a high school group in Sacramento.

The reason Ed had contacted me was that I was the director

of the 1969 high school drama group that had performed it. He thought I would appreciate the compliment, which of course I did.

Some years ago, having retired from public school teaching, I had taken various part-time college teaching jobs, and had also worked at a Sacramento record store where several of my former students were employed. One of them, the manager, hired me to work in the classical music department. Another former student, who had been a "drama groupie," said that being a part of the *Cuckoo's Nest* production and meeting Kesey at the cast party had been "one of the greatest events of my life." At the time I thought this was sort of a sad commentary on his life, and summarily dismissed it.

After thirty-five years in Sacramento, my wife and I decided to move to Santa Cruz, and my son Sean thought it would be fitting to have a going-away party, and to invite many of my former students to attend. It was during the time that we were organizing this event that I realized that *Cuckoo's Nest* was certainly one of my life's highlights also. My great salvation in teaching drama had been that I was a social science teacher who had no formal drama training at all, and I was naïve enough to think it was possible to successfully produce anything onstage. What the hell, it was just a live movie . . .

The first time I read *Cuckoo's Nest* I was much taken with the wonderful way Kesey had somehow made the "anti-institution hero" legitimate, and how readily translatable this was to the high school experience. I knew a lot of "Big Nurses" in public education who were being rewarded for their type of behavior, not only in their dealing with students but also in their manipulation of schools and administrators.

During my early drama experience with kids I began to see that they were expert in projecting melodrama, which I finally realized was an extension of their barely post-pubescent lives. Our school had little money for royalties, so I began to explore melodrama in the public domain, and of course Shakespeare and Greek tragedies were the logical choices. The kids responded with enthusiasm, and we began to produce Shakespeare, Sophocles, and Aeschylus in the round, indoor and outdoor. These efforts received surprisingly favorable reactions from both junior high and high school audiences, and after exploring a lot of classical melodrama, we had finally built up a small treasury and could afford to "do something modern." Serendipitously, I happened to hear during this time that *Cuckoo's Nest* had enjoyed only a short run on Broadway. I couldn't understand this, as it had looked like a sure winner, so I ordered a copy of the Dale Wasserman script to try to determine the reason.

After reading the script, I optimistically felt that with a quick four-letter-word rewrite, we could do this play in public school. When I approached the student drama club with the idea, they were delighted; finally, they would be able to do a play in a contemporary mode that they felt expressed their lives, especially as it pertained to people being "institutionalized." We promptly rented the script and planned production.

This was in the spring of 1969, during perhaps one of this country's greatest periods of social upheaval, and most of the kids had read the novel and easily identified with it. When the notice for tryouts went out on campus the response was overwhelming. More than three hundred students in addition to our drama club tried out for speaking parts, silent stand-ins, technical crew, publicity, etc. When a boy who stood about four feet tall and had a harelip and a speech defect tried out for the role of Billy Bibbit, I knew we had something special going! Alienated campus rebels who had shunned any and all extracurricular school activities were camped out at the drama room door during breaks, lunch, and between classes, hoping to be a part of *Cuckoo's Nest*. One kid, who had managed to alienate all his teachers, told me confidentially that he *had* to have a part in this play, as it was, he said, "the story of my life."

After casting the play, I thought of going to Oregon to see if I could find out from Kesey why the play had closed after such a short run on Broadway. As it happened, Ed McClanahan and two Kentucky writer friends of his and Kesey's were going up to Oregon for a visit, so I hitched a ride with them in Ed's VW bus.

We got to Kesey's farm in the evening and Ken's wife, Faye,

said that he was out in the field in a Cadillac, which was mired down in the mud. We approached the car in the dark, but saw no activity coming from it, and the windows were steamed over. After we'd knocked on the car's roof several times, the doors magically opened and we were pulled in by the people packed inside. Our host was in the driver's seat holding a rubber facial mask with a rubber hose attached to it. I was handed the mask, which went over the nose and mouth, and told to breathe in until I heard a bell ring, which I promptly did . . . although I don't remember hearing much else that evening. I do remember staying the night in Kesey's barn, which had been converted into a sleeping area with round holes in the walls leading to the beds. There must have been twenty to thirty guests at the farm, and most of them, it seemed, were staying in the barn, which was more like an all-night fun house. I was amazed at the speed and frequency with which people changed beds and locations.

The next few days seemed to pass very quickly, what with all the comings and goings of guests and Pranksters, but eventually I was able to talk at some length with Ken, and we agreed that this play needed to be staged so as to involve the audience as much as possible, and that light projections should be used to represent Chief Bromden's musings. These projections, as developed by Prankster Roy Sebern using overhead projectors, back-lit stencils, oil, and food coloring, were all the rage just then at rock concerts, and the kids at my school had already experimented with them at dances and various "happenings."

Meanwhile, some of the students who were later to play an integral part in the production had been expelled from school— mostly because of long hair, sideburns, or violations of the current dress code—and sent to "continuation school." But it occurred to me that because these were kids nobody else wanted anyway—the Nurse Ratcheds having done their best to get them out of their hair—their pariah status was actually an advantage, as it would allow us to get away with just about anything we cared to try.

As soon as I returned to Sacramento, we went into production seriously. The kids were incredibly focused, and they worked very hard. One cast member, for example, had to stand against the wall in a "crucified" stance throughout the entire play, which he insisted on doing during the rehearsals as well. Several times I told him to take a break, but he just smiled angelically and told me it was no problem, he was practicing his yoga.

After a couple of weeks of rehearsals, the actors who played the institutional guards began to assume the aggressive persona of real guards, so (my social science background coming out) we had to take time out to discuss the then-famous "imprisonment experiment" that had recently been conducted in the basement of Stanford University's psychology department, and the importance of treating others in a humane way—which was, after all, what the play was really about.

Meanwhile, down in Palo Alto, Ed McClanahan was trying to persuade Kesey, Roy Sebern, and assorted Pranksters to come to Sacramento to see the play. As I understand it, Kesey finally sought the advice of the I Ching, and it indicated that the trip would be auspicious.

When the kids heard that Kesey was coming they were wildly excited. Brent Smith, a friend and fellow teacher who later became a builder, had designed a "three-quarter round" set that was a real knockout. We used portable bleachers, which added to the impression that the audience was part of the institution, and during the play the guards pulled select members of the audience out of their seats, put them in straitjackets, and made them part of the silent cast as well. This seemed to go over very well with audience and cast alike, so of course when Ken, Ed, and Roy showed up we pressed them into service, too.

After the final curtain Kesey went up to the two leads during curtain call and hugged them. This brought the house down and, weirdly, without electrical manipulation, the lights seemed to come up brighter.

We ran eight weekends in Sacramento, an unheard-of record for a high school play of that era. Several weeks later I unexpectedly received a letter from Little Fox Theater in San Francisco asking if we objected to their using our set and staging ideas, as well as light projections, in their own production of *Cuckoo's Nest;* apparently, they had heard that we were doing the play, and had sent a tech representative to see it. Of course we were honored. Later, I learned that *Cuckoo's Nest* had the longest run at the Little Fox of any play in the history of San Francisco theater up to that time.

I quit teaching drama after that year; with the money *Cuckoo's Nest* had earned I wanted to do *Hair,* and the department wasn't having any. As my department chair (a retired Army major) was later heard to comment about *Cuckoo's Nest,* "Monaghan couldn't have put on a play with more communist overtones if he had wanted to."

The *Times* article about the 2001 New York production concluded as follows:

> But it was not his favorite production, Kesey added. That designation he reserved for a production he saw 30 years ago at a Sacramento high school, staged so that an elaborate display of grinding cogs and gears appeared between scenes to illustrate the play's sinister "Combine," a metaphor for society's grinding machinery.
>
> "I gave that one the A," he said.
>
> "Oh yeah?" Mr. Sinise replied, forcing a smile before thanking him for the autograph and heading back to his dressing room.
>
> "He is a character," he said.

An outtake from Mike Finoia's August 2001 interview with Kesey for Relix magazine (January 2002).

"WRONG WAY! GO BACK!"

Ken Kesey, from an
Interview with Mike Finoia

We were up once in Bellingham, Washington, and we'd gone up there to do some readings. We took the bus. Ginsberg was along. Cassady was driving. Hell of a scene. And we drove up there, and got there on Tuesday, I guess. I had to teach classes until Saturday night, when everything began to come in from everywhere. The Jefferson Airplane was the big-time lead band. This is 19—I'd say—68, maybe '67. And the bus was parked out there full of people having a wonderful time. They didn't have to get up or do anything. Cassady was just having the greatest time of his life. And finally we decided, "It's Saturday. The Jefferson Airplane is coming. We better take some acid." And we all took a good jolt of acid and we wandered into the gymnasium where it was supposed to take place. We got off the bus and the world was tipping, the cement slabs were doing this [he gestures with his hand]. We went dragging, stumbling in there. It was one of these gymnasiums with an outside ring where they have popcorn for sale and then you go through the doors to the inside where the ball games are played. We got to that outside arena, and we just couldn't figure out where we were, what was happening.

Finally, we all just kind of collapsed there on the floor, and we're sitting in the great segment there and, finally, the door opened up and this guy who at that time was the lead roadie for the Airplane. Can't remember his name. Great friend of ours. He came swirling in there and he saw us and we looked up at him and he says, "Uh-Oh!" And we nodded at him. He dragged us on in and made us a place where we could pile up there on the floor in front of the first seats. And it was completely crowded and all the lights were on. Wonderful scene. And Cassady looked out and found that audience.

"Man," he said, "There's this audience. All I need is a little hallucination."

He had on this Day-Glo driver's vest. That's all he had from the waist up. Every so often he'd bend the top of it down and put it back up and he's just twisting and having the best time. He played that audience for a good twenty minutes, and he would look at them and dance to them and he couldn't be heard. It was noisy in there.

Finally, the Airplane came out and the audience quieted down enough so they could turn off the lights and get going. The first song they played was "Somebody to Love." And, man, everything just began to happen. All these people and all the unanswered questions about what was going to happen. They changed and everything was different. Wonderful scene. Just an absolutely wonderful thing and it was spreading up. I could feel, "This is where it starts. This is where the actual millennium begins. From here on out, it will just go from one bunch of people to the next bunch of people and it will continue and it will expand and it will be understood in history. People will look back on it and all agree. Yeah, this is where it happened. This is the beginning."

At the end of the first song, Marty Balin hollered over to the guy running the soundboard and he says, "Hey! Next time you start fiddling with those dials, you'd better wait till we give you the say-so." Bring this up and that up, and suddenly his voice was so harsh and strange. And all I could think was, "Wait now. I mean, everything is about to go good on earth for a thousand years and you're arguing with this little guy about a microphone." I sat there and they sung another piece, and I couldn't get this off my mind. And they stopped the second piece. I said from the edge of the stage, "Hey Marty. You ought to apologize to that guy for getting on his case so bad." Suddenly, Cassady was all over me. Whamming me. WHOMP! WHOMP! WHOMP! And I tripped out. Suddenly I wasn't there anymore. I was up on the top of a hill outside Babbs's place in La Honda, after the Acid Test Finale. The big Acid Test Graduation. I'd gone through a tough scene there at that thing. Just barely escaped with my brain. This was the one where I told everyone we had to stop taking acid because I'd been surrounded by reporters and cops. Besides, the Hell's Angels kept coming around, sticking stuff in my mouth. Ripped to the top. And, finally, we had a get-together and worked it out. Everybody got out and sat down. Worked it out. Talked it through. There was this little guy, an amazing little guy of about eighteen, and nobody'd ever seen him before or ever again. I'd talk and he'd make these little poetic statements at the end of everything I'd say. This guy was good. He was way out beyond himself. Doubt he even remembers. I know I'll never forget it.

But anyway, Babbs took me back and he put me in this suit of clothes he had for me 'cause I was in bad shape and he straightened me up. He put me in this suit, a thing that Gretchen made for him—a really sharp green and orange outfit. And he showed me how to tuck the shirt in as a marine and how to tug it around so it was straight up and down. And he said, "Now, walk back out there." And I strolled out there. Man, I looked good. And I remember driving home when we finally got everything packed up. It was a nice sunny Sunday morning in San Francisco. At one point, I began to talk again and my mind began to unravel, and George said, "There's a sign up there that says 'Wrong Way! Go back!' " So I said, "Oh. OK."

So we go on back to Babbs's. I couldn't sleep so I headed up above Babbs's place into the hills above Santa Cruz. As I headed up his two big old hound dogs, Curly and Joe, they went up in the hills with me. And we walked and walked and finally I began to come down. I laid down and looked at Babbs's house down there. And I could see Zane, he's probably seven. He came out earlier than everyone else. He came out to Babbs's rabbit cage and crawled on top of the rabbit cage. And he's fiddling with the rabbits. I was so pleased to be there with these dogs on either side of me, so mellow and nice. I thought I'd holler at him. And I went, "Ugghrruggaah!!" This voice just came out of me and these dogs looked at me and began to pound me with their feet, and they're pounding me and beating me, and suddenly it's Cassady beating me and I was back at the Jefferson Airplane concert. And I realized I'd been through this trip, and something had taken me through and shown me, "Hey, you don't want to make these noises at this time. You want to keep quiet."

And I did. I quieted down and we sat there and watched the rest of the concert, which was a great concert, but it no longer had the chance of being the greatest concert in the history of the world. It had the door open for a second, but things got a little messy.

NO LEFT TURN UNSTONED

WITH A TIP OF THE TOPHAT TO PAUL FOSTER

Genie Murphy, Happy's amanuensis, is a writer and sometime English teacher from St. Louis. She is a long-time friend of the Kesey family.

I AM KESEY'S DOG

By Happy
(with a little help from Genie Murphy)

I AM KEN KESEY'S DOG. I saw it all, old bus, new bus. I saw a green parrot riding a ferret bareback in the living room, a joint on top of a Bible. I once saw goats dance through the back door, gambol past the couch and out the other door. I nearly coughed.

I have seen hippies with no hair and bad dogs, dread hair, multicolored hair, people just come off the road with wild desperate sweaty hair and delusional, paranoid thoughts—all were welcomed with hospitality and home movies. They ran me ragged, all the visitors. I had to protect everyone. They'd wander off by the cows and talk to them like they were porpoises, smart and communicative.

The hippie dogs wore bandanna scarves like city teenage girls and didn't seem right. When they saw ducks, they stood riveted instead of getting down low and tearing off after them. I showed them every hideyhole and every feral cat, but those dogs seemed disinterested.

The old bus is down near the pond all humble and mossy, a swamp lament. I took everyone down there to see it, famous people, Smithsonians, filmmakers from L.A., and kooks. Not one of these people ever gave me a treat.

I saw a nutria go after a feral cat near the pond, its long yellow teeth showed, and it tiptoed like a cold rat. The place is a hotbed of daily violence—the heron will shake a bullfrog in its beak like a crazy thought and gobble it down standing on one foot. The barn owl is as big as a bulldog and leaves strange messages in its dung balls, teeny bones, and fur.

When Hunter Thompson visited, he carried a pistol with him at all times. I watched over the hippies. They call me Happy.

Kesey and Texas novelist Larry McMurtry became friends in the great 1960 Stanford writing class. "Stark Gets off the Bus" is excerpted from McMurtry's article "On the Road," which appeared in The New York Review of Books, *December 5, 2002.*

✳✳✳✳✳✳✳✳✳✳✳✳✳✳✳✳✳✳✳✳✳

STARK GETS OFF THE BUS

By Larry McMurtry

The tremors struck Houston on a fine spring morning in 1964, when Ken called and said they were on a bus and were coming to see me; little did I know that the breeze of the future was about to blow through my quiet street. A very few minutes later there it came, the bus whose motto was FURTHER, and whose occupants probably indulged in a bit of drugs, sex, and rock-and-roll, as well as almost continuous movie-making and a good deal of rubbernecking as they sped across America. There were Pranksters sitting on top, waving at my startled neighbors with Day-Glo hands. Ken was playing a flute. Living legend Neal Cassady—who had inspired both *On the Road* and Allen Ginsberg's beautiful poem "The Green Automobile"—was at the wheel. My son James, aged two, was sitting in the yard in his diapers when the bus stopped and a naked lady ran out and grabbed him. It was Stark Naked (later shortened to Stark), who, being temporarily of a disordered mind, mistook him for her little girl. James, in diapers, had no objection to naked people, and the neighbors, most of them staid Republicans, took this event in stride; it was the Pranksters who were shocked.

To that point virtually every moment of the trip had been filmed, but there was Stark, wearing not a stitch, and the Pranksters were not camera-ready. I soon coached Stark inside, where she rapidly took seven showers. Neal Cassady came in, said not a word, went to sleep, and didn't stir until the next day, when it was time to leave.

The Pranksters, at this stage only on the road a few days, were extremely appealing. They were young, they were beautiful, they were fresh, and they were friendly. My neighbors at once adopted them; soon cookies were being baked and doughnuts fetched. I was glad to see the Keseys but also nervous. Who knew what Stark would do when she finished taking showers? The Kens, Kesey and Babbs, parked a mysterious jar in my kitchen cabinet—I didn't investigate but I suspect we'd all be just getting out of jail now if that jar had fallen into official hands.

I never got a solid count of Pranksters on that visit, but there were enough of them to cover most of the floor space in my small house. In the night, despite my vigilance, Stark slipped away, having no idea what city or state she was in. The police found her and at once popped her into what Carl, the Billy Bob Thornton character in *Sling Blade*, calls the "nervous hospital."

In the morning the Pranksters—who would soon be advising America to tear up their schedules and embrace spontaneity and disorder— remembered that they had a schedule: Ken's book party for *Sometimes a Great Notion* was happening in New York in only a few days. They lingered long enough for Ken to teach James his first word—"ball"—before hurrying off, Cassady again at the wheel. (In the last decade or so, touring the Northwest with his band, James has seen more of our old friends the Keseys than I have.)

This smooth departure left me, my lawyer, and Stark's lovelorn boyfriend to extract Stark from the nervous hospital. It didn't help that all our first names were Larry, but, in time, we got her out. The boyfriend was screamed at and driven off. My lawyer advised me to get her on the next plane to San Francisco, which happened to be the red-eye. In the airport, with several hours to wait, I asked her if she was hungry and she said she might eat a grilled cheese sandwich. She ate $78 worth, a big meal for an airport restaurant in 1964. As she munched she slowly regained a measure of her sanity, enough of it that when her boyfriend straggled up, the picture of woe, she meekly took his hand and got on the plane.

THE CUFF LINKS

By Ken Babbs

I could tell his duck feathers were ruffled when he walked in the office. He plopped down in his chair and didn't start telling us about the shows he had seen on TV the night before like he always did. He was definitely agitated.

"I've blown my stoic calm," he said. "Some jerks robbed our house yesterday and in broad daylight, too. We saw them running out and taking off in an old car when we got home from town. I was going to take it okay, forgiveness nine-tenths of saintliness and all that."

Yes, he said. He was going to let it ride, not get hung up. He knew the old thing about getting fixated on something. Then you got obsessed and next thing you knew you were possessed. Vengeance is mine, saith the Lord. Okay, he'd let the Lord handle it. Then he discovered his dad's cuff links were gone. That tore it. Particularly when some guy showed up later in the evening saying he'd been over to a friend's house and the friend was bragging about the burglary he'd pulled that afternoon, and it pissed this guy off when he found out whose house got robbed. He decided to come over and tell what he knew but he wouldn't say what the burglar's name was, just where he lived, in a trailer off Seavey Loop, on a dirt road, right at the first curve.

We headed out in my station wagon, my son Simon in the back seat with a wooden broom handle propped up between his legs. Someone might take it for a rifle. I grabbed the walka-round phone. It could be a walkie-talkie.

The trailer was there just as described; a real speed-freak dump. Old cars and rusted auto parts scattered in a seedy lot. Sagged mildewed singlewide. He got out the passenger side and I followed with the phone. The path was lined with canning jars filled with rocks. He banged on the screen door. No answer. He pulled it open.

"Wait a minute," I said. "You're not gonna go in there?"

Speed and guns go together like milk and cookies. He knew that. He tried the door. It was unlocked. He stooped and went inside. I put the phone to my ear and acted like I was reporting our situation. I could hear him banging around inside. Across the street there was movement in the curtains of an old farm-house.

I was getting antsy and was about to yell at him but he came out, holding his hand open. "I found them." Two round yellow cuff links engraved with his dad's initials.

A fierce old lady came striding across the street. "What do you people want? There's no one home there. You shouldn't be snooping around."

"We're Mormons, ma'am," he said, pushing past her. "You want to buy a subscription to *The Watchtower*?"

He didn't wait for an answer. We beat it out of there. He was thoughtful on the way back to the office. "A real sad scene," he said. "All the windowsills were covered with Beanie Babies. There must have been hundreds of them." He was quiet a minute. "That Beanie Baby someone left at our house. It's not there anymore. I just realized it."

A few days later the cops busted the burglar and the whole affair faded away into the lapsed memory banks and probably would have been totally forgotten except when his agent, Sterling Lord, came to Oregon for the funeral. Sterling discovered he hadn't packed his cuff links, and when Faye dug some out of the drawer to loan him the whole scary recovery operation came back in a rush.

*In the late 1950s Kesey's friend and neighbor Vic Lovell,
a graduate student in psychology at Stanford, famously
introduced Ken to the government-sponsored psycho-
tropic drug experiments then being conducted at a local
psychiatric hospital.* One Flew Over the Cuckoo's Nest *is
dedicated "To Vik Lovell who told me dragons did not exist, then led me to their lairs."*

ELEGY FOR KEN

By Vic Lovell

The men I loved in my youth have begun to die.
Once they descended like meteorites, still fresh
from other worlds, their spacy velocity
generating tremendous self-consuming heat
and the white light that contains all colors,
like opals, brightly streaking the night,
exploding like fireworks that go off in stages,
treasures of darkness, high on the sky. Watching,
my soul always jumped up to meet them.
Over and over I found myself fully alive for so brief
yet so stretched out an elastic instant. Now,
inevitably, they fall to earth.

Now they wander the streets
in their old neighborhoods,
enormous silver dinosaurs with ruby eyes
and gleaming scales. There are only a few
of us left who can still see them, but they find us;
they want to carry us on their backs,

or advise us about how to keep the faith.
Ken Kesey, I can still see the day
forty-some years ago
when you moved into the neighborhood
and it was like the holidays when colored lights appear
in trees and bushes and along the edges of roofs
and over doorways, but it was still summer.
We were agitated, but circumspect, quiet and timid.
We had a different life, invisible.
We didn't want to attract attention.
We didn't want any trouble.
And you, you pulled our covers.
You gathered strangers everywhere you went.
You made us a bohemia that proselytized,
and sometimes a great potion.
You were an escape artist: tightly bound and locked
in the ubiquitous chains of a stifling society
like Harry Houdini and you got loose (with no cheating)
and the chains fell, and lay on the ground
like dead snakes, and the crowd roared,
feeling a new freedom . . .

Two weeks ago I stood by your colorful coffin
under a big dense gray sky, looking at your body.
A nimbus flashed. I saw the Throne of Glory.
The supernal luminosity of sky-bus with you on board—
Elijah was driving but he looked just like Neal Cassady.

Sterling Lord is the distinguished literary agent who represents Kesey, Jack Kerouac, and many other noted writers. He maintains an impressive client list and is writing his memoirs.

LAST RITES

By Sterling Lord

I had spoken with Ken Kesey ten days before he went into the hospital for the operation. That was late in October 2001, and at that point, the date for the surgery hadn't been set. I had the feeling he was debating whether or not to let them cut away at his liver. He had diabetes, and hepatitis C, and in June the doctors told him he had a spot of cancer on his liver.

I had known and worked with Ken for forty years, and had last seen him on May 6 and 7, 2001. We went to the new Broadway revival of *One Flew Over the Cuckoo's Nest*, and he stayed overnight with my wife, Meg, and me. He was already showing some of the effects of disease, and David Stanford, his longtime editor and friend, with whom Ken had been staying for a week or so, later told me I had seen Ken during an improved period. He had just stopped taking Interferon after several months on the medication, which had been very hard on him. Even so, he was a pleasure to be with, as always.

Once he'd had the operation, his closest friend, Ken Babbs, who lives in Dexter, Oregon, not far from Kesey's farm, and David Stanford kept me up to speed on his condition. Babbs called to tell me the doctor was letting Kesey out. At first it seemed he was being discharged, but then it turned out to be just for the afternoon. (Ken went to visit the farm.) Toward the end of the second week it began to look ominous. When I talked to David at his home in upstate New York on Thursday, November 8, he had already booked a flight to Eugene for the following day.

On Saturday morning, November 10, since I had heard nothing further, I set out early to do some errands in midtown Manhattan, planning to stop at the office later that morning to get David Stanford's home number. I knew his wife, Therese, who was at home, would have any late word from Oregon. She did: Ken had died around 4:30 A.M. while family and friends, faithfully sitting in the hospital waiting room, had dozed off.

I phoned Meg immediately and learned Babbs had called her at home to try to get the news to me. It was 11:10 A.M. in New York. By noon I had made plane reservations, called Faye to ask if it was all right to come (she was pleased that I was coming), packed my bag, arranged to have the air tickets delivered to our apartment, called for a car, and was on the way to JFK for a 2:45 flight to Eugene via San Francisco. I accomplished most of the above with Meg's thoughtful and efficient assistance. Since it was post 9/11, I was trying to get to JFK two hours in advance, in accordance with the new rules.

"We're at war," Meg reminded me. (We live in Greenwich Village, not far from Ground Zero.) "There will be men in army uniforms with machine guns. I haven't packed any nail clippers. They'll stop you for that."

Arriving in Eugene at 8:50 P.M., I was met by Faye and David, an extraordinarily thoughtful and gracious act since it was still the day Ken died. They guided me to my motel in downtown Eugene, and even came in for a chat. Faye rode with me in my rental car and in her quiet voice she explained that the hospital had taken extremely good care of Ken.

The next morning being Sunday, Faye and David were to go to church. I drove out to the farm, following Faye's written instructions. It was a beautiful sunny day, with a high clear sky, and the Pleasant Hill area in the Willamette valley looked gorgeous, as I'd remembered it from my visit five years earlier. The view from Kesey's huge living room window looking down the verdant valley, with the low-lying mountain ranges staggered in the distance, is rich and soul-satisfying.

I walked around the grounds, looked into the bus barn, and there stood the huge International Harvester Further, in which Ken had generously transported me to the airport at the end of my stay in 1996. I wandered around to the other side of the house and saw that there were no animals or fowl around the tiny lake, as there had been at the time of my earlier trip, but of course it was almost winter now, and the water level was way down. In the field in front of the house, I saw the low-slung hay wagon, the one I had fallen from one night in 1996. Faye and I had been tossing off bales of hay to the cows as Ken, driving the tractor, pulled us slowly around in circles.

"It's the first time I've ever seen you when you weren't in total control," Ken told me at breakfast the next morning.

We were sitting at the great round table in the Kesey kitchen, near the picture window that looks out over the cow pasture.

"Look," I said to Ken, pointing to the very spot where I had fallen, "the cows are all gathered around the spot where I fell, as if to commemorate the fall."

I heard later that Ken had been telling that story, with some minor embellishments, over the years since.

But this Sunday, the day after Ken's passing, I walked around and got up on the hay wagon just to relive that incident, to see how far I had really fallen. It wasn't far. The story had profited from the distance halo: the farther away in time or geographical distance, the more a story is likely to grow.

The strength and size of the Kesey family soon became apparent. Although I had met many of them, including Ken's mother, Geneva, in 1963 when they all came east for the opening of the original stage production of *Cuckoo's Nest*, I didn't get the full picture until now.

Shortly after noon, as Faye and David returned from church, family members and neighbors started dropping in, bringing a great variety of food. A buffet lunch continued through the afternoon, served and managed by the women.

Faye and Ken's daughter Shannon Smith; her mother-in-law, Elaine; son Zane and his wife, Stephanie; daughter Sunshine and her mother, Mountain Girl; Geneva and her husband, Ed Jolley; brother Chuck, his wife, Sue; their daughter Cheryl and son Kit; and many others were there, as was Ken Babbs, of course. There was a wonderful feeling of warmth and good will.

There were no tears, no sad faces. I think it was the way Ken would have wanted it, a quiet celebration of his life.

The service was set for Wednesday, November 14, at the Mc-Donald Theatre in downtown Eugene, a former movie house where Ken had appeared on stage in his early days. The theater is now under long-term contract to Ken's nephew Kit Kesey. Kit has restored the theater beautifully, and had only recently re-opened it for concerts, movies, and other events. But since Sunday, when the McDonald was selected, Babbs had been worried that the theater would not be large enough to hold the crowd. And because Babbs had been with Ken so long, through so many performances, I took his concerns seriously even though I knew the theater could seat 750 people.

But Sunday night Babbs had a dream and in that dream Kesey appeared and said to him, "What do you mean the Mc-Donald can't accommodate the crowd. Put loudspeakers in the street!" And that's what they did, to accommodate a total attendance of 1,000 persons, as reported in all the newspapers the next day.

Somewhere in the first days of the week Ed McClanahan showed up, from Lexington, Kentucky, as did Bob Faggen, a professor at Claremont College who had interviewed Kesey for *The Paris Review*, as well as two of the students from Kesey's famous University of Oregon writing class—probably the only academic group in the history of literature who put together a novel written by thirteen people (*Caverns*, Penguin, 1989). Mc-Clanahan had been Kesey's friend since the Perry Lane days of the early 1960s, and I had admired his writing and was pleased to meet him. I had met Faggen at the farm five years before when Ken introduced him to me as the writer he wanted to write his biography. Both wanted me to be Bob's agent.

On Monday morning, Stephanie brought David and me to the Special Collections section of the University of Oregon Library, so we could look through the voluminous collection of Kesey manuscripts and materials. Stephanie introduced us to James Fox, the Director of Special Collections and University Archives, who could not have been more courteous and helpful in receiving us. I had been there before with Ken. It's an impressive room and Kesey's material is well taken care of. Going through the files, I marveled at how much writing Ken had done in his lifetime, in addition to all that living.

On Tuesday, Ed, Stephanie, and I drove out to Chuck and Sue's Springfield Creamery, near the airport. There we found a group that included Zane, Kit, Chuck, George Walker, John Swan, and George Braddock, a family friend who had constructed a beautiful white wooden coffin. There was a large aluminum vat filled with water, upon which Zane poured many colors of oil paint. Together they carefully dipped the coffin into the vat. The whole proceeding had a feeling of ritual solemnity despite the customary Prankster bonhomie. The coffin emerged psychedelically marbeled with beautiful pastel colors.

The next day the Kesey women started cutting and sewing together some colorful lengths of silk Ken had bought in China to make the lining for the casket.

Monday and Tuesday had been what Oregonians regarded as typical winter days, overcast, gloomy, and with intermittent rain. Wednesday started the same way, but midway through the morning, as if to herald the noontime funeral services, the sun broke through. Intermittently at first, but it was there.

The services had been scheduled for noon to accommodate many of Faye's friends who worked in downtown Eugene and could only leave work during their lunch hour. Accordingly, the service was scheduled to last no more than two hours, and indeed it didn't.

The theater was tightly packed by noon, and two musician friends of Kesey's, Art Maddox (on piano) and Steve Schuster (on many instruments) were playing on the stage, next to the multicolored coffin. Later, they would be joined by another great friend of Kesey's, the composer Mason Williams.

The family had carefully planned the ceremony over the previous few days. David Stanford had designed the program and he and his cousin, Karen Sublette, printed it at Kinko's late the night before. In light of the two-hour limit, those of us who were to speak were told to keep to our allotted times.

Earlier that week, when I was asked if I wanted to speak at the service, I had declined. I was overwhelmed by the dignity and strong presence of the Kesey family, and thought I might be intruding. But David knew the scene and the family, and he convinced me that it was the right thing to do.

"I need a title!" he demanded. So I called it "The Writer and the Man." I was already thinking of the phone call I had made on Sunday morning to my daughter Rebecca, who lives in St. Petersburg, Florida. She had first met Ken when she was five years old, had seen him again when she was twelve; then about ten years ago she was with me when I saw Ken in Toronto. She had just heard of Ken's death an hour before I called, and was very sad.

"Dad," she said over the phone, "whenever I was with Ken Kesey I felt safe and loved. It was as if his heart was reaching out to touch my heart."

And that's the way I concluded my speech. Earlier in the week at the farm I had told that story to one of the Kesey men and his response was, "But isn't that the way we all felt!"

David followed me by reading from *Sometimes a Great Notion* (near the end of the service he read a second section) but neither of us exceeded five minutes. Zane's film of Ken in action was longer, and quite wonderful, but the all-time not-to-be-forgotten speech, under the title "Let's Make This Short," was by Ken Babbs, who spoke for around an hour. He covered everything from poignant memories of adventures he and Kesey had shared to the fact that I had come out from New York without my cuff links and Faye had saved the day by lending me a pair given to Kesey years ago by his father.

At the end of the service, the eight pallbearers climbed on-stage, shouldered the coffin, and carried it through the crowd out onto Willamette Street where Further was parked and wait-ing, and loaded it onto the rear platform of the bus. Kesey fans, some of whom had followed the coffin out of the theater and others who had heard the services through the loudspeakers on the street, crowded around the bus before it chugged off on its way to the farm.

Photo by Barbara Wolpman

Ken had wanted to be buried on the farm, the land he cher-ished, on a low rise that offered a beautiful long view down the valley in either direction. The spot he chose was beside the grave of his son Jed, who died in 1984 in an accident when the Uni-versity of Oregon wrestling team bus went over a cliff en route to a match.

The day after his passing, Ken's family and friends, led by Kit Kesey, had started digging the grave. It wasn't until I was down in the hole, shovel in hand, that I realized what an extraordinary thing was happening—that Ken's remains would stay, hopefully forever, on the land he loved, next to his deceased son, in a grave dug by family and extended family. A member of the family told me that Ken had wanted to ensure that the land would stay in the family forever. However, since that was not possible legally, this was the next best move.

By Tuesday a large white tent, large enough to cover the grave as well as fifty or sixty folding chairs, was in place. That was the destination of Further with the coffin. The burial service was for family only, but by the time I reached the farm in my rental car, the field in front of the home was crowded with cars, and the driveway was full. The Kesey women and family friends were serving a buffet lunch in the living room/kitchen. Soon, people started wandering out to the gravesite where Ken's casket was on a metal support base at the head of the grave. Later, as the sun was going down and all hands were under the tent, there was an informal service. Half a dozen persons spoke and then we filed past the open coffin to see the lifeless Ken in his purplish-red beret.

Faye was seated in the front row, and once the casket was lowered into the ground, many of the men, women, and children took turns shoveling dirt back into the grave, covering the coffin, while others filed by to pay their respects to Faye. Both David and I participated in the shoveling, though we were not the heaviest lifters. By the time darkness began to fall, the grave was completely filled and Ken had been permanently laid to rest.

The headstone, bearing the engraved words "Sparks Fly Upward," was yet to be put in place, but the sparks were surely already flying.

On February 11, 2001, writers Robert Stone, Tom Wolfe, and Ed McClanahan, and Kesey's editor David Stanford (l. to r. below) participated together in a tribute to Kesey at New York's 92nd Street Y, a national literary forum for more than a hundred years. Wolfe, who is also a caricaturist and amateur calligrapher, devoted his portion of the program to a synopsis, with commentary, of The Electric Kool-Aid Acid Test. *His notes for the presentation are reproduced on the following pages. Stone's remarks appear on p. 198.*

✳✳✳✳✳✳✳✳✳✳✳✳✳✳✳✳✳✳✳✳✳✳

"IN THE PUDDING"

By Tom Wolfe

February 11 ① 2002

◎ AS JOURNALIST ∴ The FUGITIVE

◎ SNEAKS BACK ∴ "SALT In
J. EDGAR'S WOUNDS" ∴ ARREST

PRANKSTERS:
◎ JAIL INTERVIEW ∴ "UNSPOKEN
"THE CHIEF"   THING"

① THE PARABLE ● RELIG
INTO
THE MOVIE   CHARISMATIC   21-25   W/ LSD
            ANTI-SMALL-TALK
◎ NOT UNUSUAL ∴ WACHB
PARTISAN RUBRIC ∴ NOT THEOLOGY
BUT THE EXPERIENCE ∴
THE KAIROS ● 14-15 ③ (13-14)
◎ NOT ONLY KESEY "IN
THE
PUDDING!"

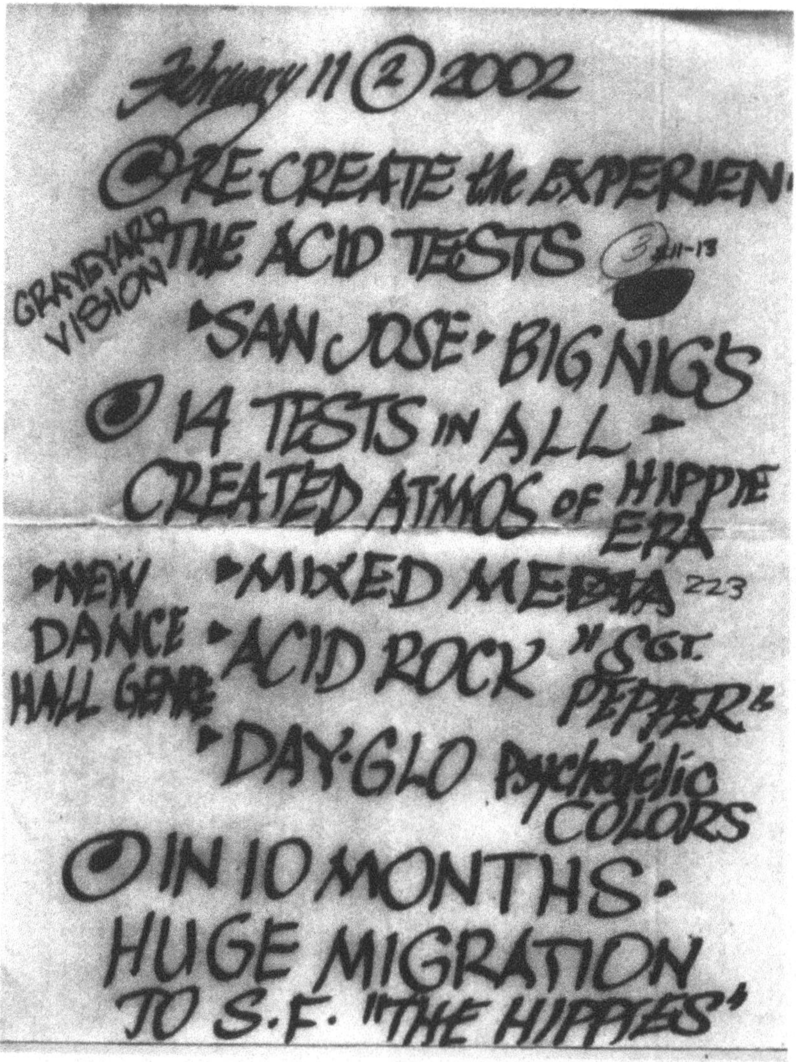

February 11 ② 2002

⊙ RE-CREATE the EXPERIEN-
GRAVEYARD VISION THE ACID TESTS ③ ₈₋₁₁₋₁₃
• SAN JOSE • BIG NIGS
⊙ 14 TESTS IN ALL •
CREATED ATMOS of HIPPIE ERA
• NEW   • MIXED MEDIA ²²³
DANCE   • ACID ROCK " Sgt.
HALL GENRE   PEPPER "
            • DAY-GLO Psychodelic COLORS

⊙ IN 10 MONTHS •
HUGE MIGRATION
TO S.F. "THE HIPPIES'

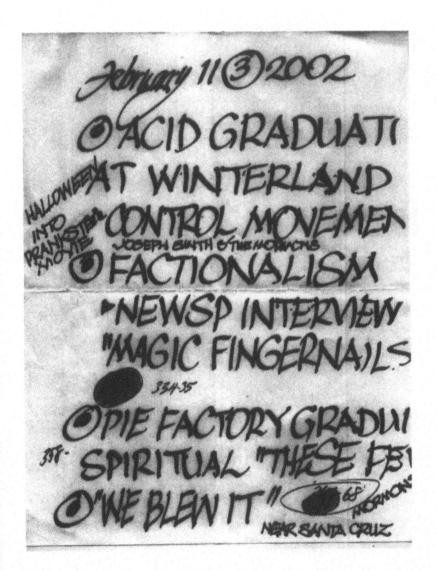

February 11 ③ 2002

⊙ ACID GRADUATI
HALLOWEEN AT WINTERLAND
INTO
PRANKSTER ⊙ CONTROL MOVEMEN
MOVIE   JOSEPH SMITH & THE MORMONS
⊙ FACTIONALISM
➤ NEWSP INTERVIEW
"MAGIC FINGERNAILS.
● 334-35
⊙ PIE FACTORY GRADUI
338- SPIRITUAL "THESE FB!
⊙ "WE BLEW IT" ● 364-68
MORMONS
NEAR SANTA CRUZ

123

"So let's set here in this dilapidated people hutch and think about the things we've done..."

"...Yes...down in Mississippi, that bitch girl we diddled in the cotton fields..."

"Still...you want to catch the first subway to Heaven..."

"If I can get myself a new set of scales, I'll get my ass off this third rail...and so saying, he stood up and retched and looked down on the rail on spurls and long and hairy slavers of various flavors of dark intestinal brown..."

"...and his teeth fell out by the dozen and Hitler and his infested cousins began to grow in the cellar like a new hybrid corn and the crows wouldn't touch him..."

"...and up the rail, old True Blue wiped his nose on his uncle's clothes..."

"I took some pseulobin and one long diddle..."

"WE BLEW IT!"

"...Ten thousand times or more.."

"WE BLEW IT!"

"...so much we can't keep score..."

"WE BLEW IT!"

"...just when you're beginning to think, 'I'm going to score'..."

"WE BLEW IT!"

"...but there's more in store..."

"WE BLEW IT!"

"...if we can get rid of these trading stamps that get in the way of the merchandise..."

"WE BLEW IT!"

"...Ten million times or more!..."

"WE BLEW IT!"

"...it was perfect, so what do you do?..."

"WE BLEW IT!"

"...perfect!..."

"WE BLEW IT!"

EPILOGUE

Three weeks later, November 30, Kesey we_ Francisco for possession of marijuana—the b_ top. It ended with a hung jury, split 8 t_ Kesey's retrial, in April, ended with ano_ 11 to 1 against him this time. Rather than_ however, the state let him plead nolo conte_ charge, "_____ b___ th_ p_ace where_ _ _ _ _ for ___ _ _ _ out in b_ San M____ _ _tion fo_ marijuana—the La Honda bust. __ _ _ence _ _ _ _ _ _ concurrently, __ _ _d th_ other s_ _ _ _ _ _ _ _ _ _ _ _ _ _ _ _ _ l_ _ _ _ _ _ _ _d, O_ F_ _ _ Lee and Ram Rod on board._ pretty much scatter_ _ _ _ _ in Mexico ___ _ ___ ready joined _ ___ _teful_ Paul Foster went to the Hog Farm, Hugh_ mune near Los A_ _ Babbs and Gretch w_ _ _ _ _ _ _ _ By J_ _, Kesey _ _ his stretch on the w_ was just a few miles from his old place in _ worked in the tailor shop. He was let out after serving five months. He went back to _ and Faye set up house in a shed on his b_ farm, up a gravel road south of Springfield. called the Space Heater House after a gas h_

OFAILED, BUT C'V BEEN LIKE THE MORMONS

OMOST EXTRAORDINARY WRITER RUN INTO

"Anonymous" (Linda Breen) lives in Eugene, and is working on her memoirs. Rick Dodgson is a Ph.D. candidate in history at Ohio University's Contemporary History Institute, and is writing his dissertation on Kesey and the Pranksters. He interviewed Anonymous on July 11, 2001.

"CAN I GO WITH YOU?"

Anonymous Gets on the Bus

From an Interview with Rick Dodgson

Anonymous was just fifteen when she first got "On the Bus" at the Calgary Stampede in 1964. In the interview segment below, "Anon" (as she is known to this day among her Prankster friends) recalls her first encounter with the Pranksters—in which she acquired her indelible nickname—and her spontaneous decision to join them on the return leg of their now-famous trip to New York. What struck me most about this interview was that she recalled emotions and sensations far more clearly than she did times and dates and places and all those other details best left to nervous historians. Her memories serve to remind us of what a bewildering sensory experience it must have been for an impressionable fifteen-year-old to run across that old multicolored school bus and its weird load in a remote, wild-west Canadian town in the pre-psychedelic era.—R.D.

Rick Dodgson: Tell me the story of how you first met [the Pranksters].

Anonymous: It was at the Calgary Stampede . . .

RD: That would be August 1964?

Anon: No, July. Everybody [at home] was gone. It was the summer holidays. It was a horrible, oppressing day. It was hot and sunny. Nobody was home. I was just lonely, depressed. The guy I liked, his girlfriend came back. [Laughs.] So I took the bus to the Calgary Stampede. I was by myself, I had gone into the grounds, and the Calgary Stampede is just the biggest thing, all the rides, so I was just kicking around, literally scuffling around seeing if there was anyone I knew. Not even in a good mood.

RD: I don't even know what the Calgary Stampede is. Is it a rodeo, or . . . ?

Anon: Yes, one of the biggest rodeos, biggest carnivals in the world! If you go in the morning they have chuck wagon breakfasts, you can have pancakes, eggs, and bacon for almost nothing, fifty cents and you got this huge breakfast. It's kinda like the Eugene Country Fair, only on a Western theme, square dances in the streets and people fiddle-playing, it was just wild and crazy. I remember it was just packed, just people-to-people, going to the fairgrounds, getting in. And then there was the Bus . . .

They had just crazy-painted it. There was no rhyme, no reason to the painting. There were no [images of] people on it, just spray paint here, then spray paint there, and it had a balcony on top, and instruments and people hanging all over, Gretchen was like hanging, her legs swinging, leaning over the rail with her hat on, and people were blowing flutes and there were drums hanging there, and people dancing all around. They were getting ready to go. But if you know the Pranksters, it takes them a long time to get going.

RD: Were they just "being," or were they performing?

Anon: Just "Oh this is fun, whoohoo, let's do this!" You know, it was never quite a performance, but you'd find that when you're cutting up and people stop and look at you, then you cut up more, and then pretty soon you've got everyone cutting up with you, and it's just one big scene, one big gig. They were just cutting up and getting ready to go, and they were fascinating people, absolutely fascinating people. Everybody smiled and I wasn't smiling, I wasn't happy, my heart was whatever a fifteen-year-old's heart is, and I just had to be away from where I was. And I asked them, "Can I go with you?" after standing there and staring for quite a while. They were smiling at me, I was shy. "Can I go with you?" And Hagen . . . [Laughs.]

RD: The book [*The Electric Kool-Aid Acid Test*] has it that you were . . .

127

Anon: One of Hagen's girls. [Laughs.] Come on, they thought I was older than I was.

RD: Were you a "Western Frontier Chick" or a "Beatnik Babe" at this time?

Anon: Beatnik. I don't know why I got into the Beatnik thing. When I went Halloweening I wore Dad's white shirt and my Capris, I was cool. Whatever it was, I don't know, I fell into that category because I just spent a lot of time with just me and my dog, alone, a lot, a lot, a lot.

RD: Can you remember thinking, is this a circus troupe, or just a strange bunch of people, or . . . ?

Anon: I didn't label them at all, I've never been much for labels in my life. I just thought they looked like fun, and I didn't see any reason . . . I don't think I was thinking, like, "I'm gonna take off and I'm gonna run away from home, I'm gonna get away from this." It was just "Can I go with you?" They just made me feel so good. You have to remember I was feeling really bad, and I don't know what it was about them, they just made me feel good. They let me on the bus, and just pulling out of the whole crowd, there's hundreds and thousands of people, and the bus slowly getting out of there, by the time we got out onto Eighth Avenue toward the exit out of town it was dark, it was fading out. And by then— I wasn't smoking, I was straight, I was me—I had my face painted, I think I was in my bra and pants—I was always in my bra and pants—and I was feeling good. The police stopped the bus on the road, right in the middle of Eighth Avenue. They had a school picture of me, and were asking whether I was on the bus. And I'm looking, and here's the cops right here [gestures below her], and I'm cheeky as hell, looking over their shoulders, my face all painted, and I'm saying "Who'd want to find *her*?" By then my whole character of morose, sad little fifteen-year-old was just gone. And it just went right over their heads.

RD: So you were having no second thoughts?

Anon: I wasn't thinking, I wasn't even having *first* thoughts. I just knew I was there, it was like it was meant to be, there was no question that being inside the bus and on the bus was a normal and natural part of my life. I just had to follow that path, and just one step and there I was.

John Daniel lives in the Coast Range foothills north of Noti, Oregon. His latest book is Winter Creek: One Writer's Natural History. *"The Prankster Moves On" originally appeared in* Open Spaces Quarterly.

THE PRANKSTER MOVES ON

By John Daniel

Ken Kesey was dressed in white from head to toe when I first encountered him, at a writers conference a friend and I had organized in Klamath Falls in 1979. A broad, powerful man, he talked at dinner about farming and especially about sheep, the purity of their innocence, how we needed that in our lives. There was a Christian flavor in his remarks. He likened himself to a retired country squire. I, tuned to his every word with the hunger of an unrecognized novice, was duly disappointed. This was my psychedelic hero, the progenitor of McMurphy and Stamper, the Prankster-in-Chief on the bus called "Furthur"?

But in the fiction workshop he said some things I've never forgotten. He asked what we were reading. "You!" somebody said. Well, Kesey came back, you shouldn't be reading me. If you want to write you should be reading Melville and Hawthorne, Shakespeare, the King James Bible. You should go to the source. Listen, he said, his enthusiasm gathering, when you sit down to write you're inside a bubble, see? And the bubble grows outside of time, outside your little room, and with you in that bubble are the greatest writers—if you know them. That's the possibility, the pure potential of writing, he told us.

On the second day, perhaps a bit worn down by short stories such as mine, which was about a man who kills a woman and forgets it and climbs a mountain and remembers and freezes to death, Kesey said, "People, listen. It comes down to this. If it doesn't uplift the human heart, piss on it."

He was then forty-four. For twelve years he had been living on the farm near Pleasant Hill where he had grown up in the 1940s and '50s, doing magic acts onstage at the McDonald Theater in Eugene, wrestling for the University of Oregon and almost making the 1960 Olympic team. Between growing up and resettlement came ten years during which Ken Kesey's name blazed into national fame and notoriety.

Soon after enrolling in Wallace Stegner's Stanford University creative writing program in 1958, which changed his life, Kesey enrolled in a very different curriculum that also changed his life—Army-sponsored tests at a VA hospital on the effects of psychoactive drugs, for which he received $75 a session: He became an instant advocate of exploring the inner wilderness of the psyche, and changing society, by means of LSD. When he hired on as a night aide in the psychiatric ward of the hospital, he recognized the kinship between psychedelic awareness and psychosis—the patients were lost explorers. He began a story about life in just such a ward, a story that wouldn't cohere until one night, in a peyote-induced vision, Kesey conjured a schizophrenic Indian he called Chief Bromden. He had a narrator and a novel.

The miracle of *Cuckoo's Nest* is, first, that a guy could write a novel while regularly blasting his head with hallucinogens, and second, that he could write a very fine novel in which psychedelic awareness, deftly and aptly incorporated, is essential to the tale. Kesey had the strength to harness for his art the experience that reduced most of us to wordlessness. He captures its paranoid aura in the subtle click and hum of machinery Chief Bromden hears in the asylum walls, and in the "microscopic wires and grids and transistors . . . designed to dissolve on contact with air" the Chief finds when be crushes one of the daily sedatives Big Nurse force-feeds her inmates. And he evokes just as tellingly the expansive, synesthetic happiness of the psychedelic high, as when Randle Patrick McMurphy first enters and bellows his vast laugh—"it's free and loud and it comes out of his wide grinning mouth and spreads in rings bigger and bigger till it's lapping against the walls all over the ward."

The miracle occurred, it turns out, in the ordinary way—through hard work. According to Malcolm Cowley, the Stanford teacher Kesey liked best, he wrote long patches of the book "at top speed," often under the influence, but returned to those drafts later to add, delete, correct, and rewrite, responding to Cowley's observations and his own sober judgment. The canard that Kesey never revised his first drafts, in the fashion of the Beats, has survived too long.

Cuckoo's Nest, tapping perfectly the temper of the times with its cosmology of a tight-assed freedom-hating Combine running the country, was published in 1962 to enormous acclaim. Hard on its heels two years later came a second novel, *Sometimes a Great Notion*. Kesey returned to Oregon, lived in logging camps, and refrequented the haunts of his youth to write it. *Cuckoo's Nest* is the better-achieved book, but *Notion* may be the greater achievement—a sprawling, boisterous, multigenerational story of a Coast Range logging family pitted against its community, one brother locking horns with another, and East Coast culture at odds with earthy Western stubbornness, these tensions playing out in a place—landscape, weather, biota—as intimately evoked as any in literature. If *Cuckoo's Nest* shines with the moral clarity of parable, *Notion* has the variegated texture, heroic proportions, and moral complexity of epic myth. The book's ambition is evident in the method of its telling, in which time slides freely backward and forward and point of view slips continually among several characters and an eerie, Whitmanian omniscient observer who sees everything, right down to blackberry roots deepening their hold in the rain-sodden earth.

Sometimes a Great Notion sometimes trips on its special effects. It is verbose, overlong, and in parts overwritten. And it is, like *One Flew Over the* Cuckoo's Nest, one of the best novels I know.

"I don't think I'll ever be able to do that again," Kesey told an interviewer, and he wasn't. Two books in two years seemed to exhaust his verbal artistry, or maybe only redirected it. As the first (very mixed) reviews of *Notion* appeared in 1964, Kesey and his band of Merry Pranksters were cavorting cross-country in a 1939 International Harvester school bus they had lushly painted with dazzling Day-Glo colors, dropping acid, filming a movie, and demonstrating to the heartland—offering the heartland—their version of the new consciousness. Back in California they spread the news through the Acid Tests, serving up LSD—still perfectly legal—in smoking punchbowls of Kool-Aid on dry ice, as strobe lights flickered and colored lights pulsed on the dance hall walls to the music of a new band called the Grateful Dead.

But if he was an avatar of "Better Living Through Chemistry," Kesey quickly came to see some of its limits. A final Acid Test, on Halloween night, 1966, was meant to convey to the faithful that it was time to move beyond the frequent use of psychedelics. Kesey, already in trouble with the law on a marijuana charge, eventually served six months in the San Mateo County jail. On his release he came home to Oregon and his father's farm, where he settled in with Faye, the high school sweetheart he had married in 1956, to raise their children.

He now wrote magazine pieces, mainly, many of them elegiac about what the counterculture had been and rueful about what it was becoming—violence at rock concerts, hard drug use, stars such as Janis Joplin and Jim Morrison and Jimi Hendrix dropping dead from overdoses. Kesey scuttled a Prankster plan to drive the bus cross-country again, to the Woodstock music festival, and soon afterward wrote a story called "The Day After Superman Died." The reference is to Neal Cassady, the legendary "Fastestmanalive," hero of Jack Kerouac's *On the Road* and driver of Furthur on the Pranksters' 1964 trek. In the story Kesey has a tense standoff with two hippies who drop in at the farm on their way home from Woodstock, a young airhead and an older, tattooed, rotten-toothed, Mansonesque jerk. The atmosphere is all irony and apocalypse—a pall of acrid smoke from burning fields, Kesey unable to find his "colored glasses," a young lamb inexplicably dead, the Beach Boys singing "Good Vibrations" on a tinny radio, then a friend arriving with news that Cassady, doped-up in Mexico, has died of exposure on an expedition to count railroad ties.

In the same story, Kesey's conservative friend Larry McMurtry asks in a letter, "What has the Good Old Revolution been doing lately?"

"Losing," is all Kesey can think to reply.

Or changing form, moving on to the next stage. Kesey parked the bus, cranked up his tractor, and acquired a small fleet of long, low convertibles for working the farm. He applied himself to the raising of cattle and sheep and the growing of blueberries. As his kids went through the Pleasant Hill schools he served on school board committees. He coached wrestling, cheered for both sides at football games. He spoke, whenever asked, at rural high school commencement ceremonies. He used his stature in various ways to help out local businesses. For more than three decades he lived a life of engagement with family and community, a life that offers very lean pickings to those who would tag him as an irresponsible misleader of youth.

Kesey showed himself to be, in the best and most basic sense of the term, a conservative. He did not renounce psychedelic drugs or his distrust of power and authority or his flair for outrageous antics. He most certainly did not renounce the essential '60s vision that valued community over corporate profits, peace and tolerance over war and fearfulness, a sense of life's beauty and mystery over the customary trappings of career, money, and piles of possessions. He conserved what was best in the cultural upheaval he had so boldly assisted and melded it into the traditional culture he had grown up in and returned to. He planted his values in place and community, even as Furthur, the original bus, sank slowly into a swale on his farm, young trees growing up around it.

Kesey even taught for a year at the University of Oregon, violating his own youthful judgment about what he had learned at Stanford from Wallace Stegner: "Just never to teach in college." He and Stegner had clashed from the beginning, inevitably, perhaps, given their differences, the one a brash drug-taking rebel buzzing with Beat energy, the other a liberal of conservative temperament who had taught at Harvard and founded the writing program at Stanford. Stegner saw Kesey as talented but undisciplined, a wastrel. "I was never sympathetic to any of his ideas," Stegner recalled years later, "because I thought many of his ideas were half-baked." Kesey saw Stegner as the epitome of academic staidness and convention. "When we headed off on a bus to deal with the future of our synapses," Kesey remarked in 1993, "we knew that Wally wasn't liking what we were doing and that was good enough for us."

Stanford, as the 1950s turned into the '60s, had the strongest concentration of writing talent in its history: Robert Stone, Ernest Gaines, Larry McMurtry, Tillie Olsen, Ed McClanahan, Ken Babbs, and Wendell Berry, among others, shared the oval seminar table with Kesey and Stegner. Most of them appreciated both men. "Stegner saw Kesey as a threat to civilization and intellectualism and sobriety," Robert Stone told Stegner's biographer. "And Ken was a threat to all those values. But what was going on around Ken was so exciting that we were not about to line up against each other on ideological grounds."

Both men in later years felt that too much had been made of their fractious relationship. "We got along in class perfectly swell," Stegner told his biographer. "I liked his writing most of the time very well." And Kesey, when I asked him once if Stegner had been a good teacher, replied, "He was better than a teacher. He was like Vince Lombardi, and we were the Green Bay Packers of fiction writing." The trouble between them, I think now, may have stemmed as much from their likeness as it did from their differences. Each made his way to literary fame from inauspicious beginnings in the rural West, and each arrived with an attitude stamped into his soul. Stegner's was: When you start with nothing you'd better work, work, work. Kesey's was: Watch out or high culture will suck out your life.

There's validity in both.

The Green Bay Packers of fiction stayed variously bonded

over the decades. It was with Wendell Berry and his wife, in November of 2000, that my wife and I tagged along to visit the Keseys at their farm. Kesey and Ken Babbs, close sidekicks and neighbors for forty-two years, got the bus—son of Furthur, or son of son of Furthur—coughing to life with a few shots of starting fluid, and another Prankster drove it creepingly out of its shed. (A fitting emblem, it seemed, for the persistence of the '60s in our lives.) We admired its zany, mysterious, brightly painted figures. Kesey circled the bus, presenting it with pride. A year later it would bear him in his hand-painted casket to his memorial service at the McDonald Theater, and then, its bell tolling, to his grave on the farm.

Photo by Kit Andrews

Fay and Ken, c. 1985

In the warmth of the Keseys' barn-become-house, accompanied by several Pranksters and members of the Kesey family, the old friends visited. Berry observed that of all the Green Bay Packers, only he and Kesey remained married to their wives of that time. Kesey, though bulging in the middle at age sixty-five, was still recognizable as Malcolm Cowley described him in

1960, with "the build of a plunging halfback, big shoulders and a neck like the stump of a Douglas fir." As I watched him something came to me. I had been one of the many who waited impatiently through the '70s and '80s for a new novel, an even better novel, and I was one of the many who were disappointed in the books he eventually did produce. What a measly, impertinent attitude that was. As if writing two of the best American novels of the century and lighting up our times with his verve and enthusiasm had not been enough. As if he owed us, when in truth we all owed him.

We ate at two round oak tables. At mine, as Ken Babbs riffed, laughing his laugh of absolute commitment to the wonder and pleasure of living, the Prankster-in-Chief looked very much the country squire—at home in his chair, pleased with the company, making sure that wineglasses were filled when they needed to be filled and that all present had seconds and a fair shot at thirds of the great slab of salmon Faye had baked. It was a fine feast, and so was Ken Kesey's life, and I am grateful for all he served.

"Earthshoes" is an address to the Eugene, Oregon, Friends of the Library in 1976. It appeared with "Karma (and Other Sermons)" (see p. 36) in The Co-Evolution Quarterly *(Spring 1976).*

EARTHSHOES

By Ken Kesey

There's a phrase in Egypt for something that is sold in the marketplace. Here's a pot that's made out of brass and here's another made out of brass. They're the same pot. This one is old and beat up; this one's brand new. The old one sells for more money. It's said that it has baracca; it means that it's been blessed; just the amount of hands that have touched it, the amount of eyes that have looked at it, have blessed it in some way and made it magic. You can tell what's good by how worn it is. That isn't the way our aesthetics are headed.

As everyone knows, people aren't reading as well as they did when we were younger, for a number of reasons. There is a "Sesame Street"–"Welcome Back, Kotter" consciousness that has crept in not only to our homes but into our schools and into our libraries. And gradually as these trendy things that I call "earthshoes" work their way in, something good drops off at the end, until finally what you're left with is a lot of fashion and nothing that's eternal. This is the point of a library, whether it's my little bookbag here, or the big library in Eugene, or the University of Oregon library which I'm familiar with and use frequently. It is where you house the eternal that you've gathered.

I have here a bunch of books that I picked up both from

around my place and from the high school. Here's *Grapes of Wrath* by John Steinbeck. It's been around a lot; it's a sturdy book. It was put out—let's see when it was put out—'39. That book will stand up another forty years. It could have another thousand eyes pass over it. The book wouldn't be harmed and every eye would be benefited. This is one of my books.

These are some of the books I picked up from the high school reading room. I picked them up according to how they were worn. This is how you know what's being read. This is *Nigger*, by Dick Gregory, which cries out to be read like a lot of the trendy ethnic or feminist or earthshoe literature does, to the detriment of really good, say, female writers or black writers—good writers like H.D., Hilda Doolittle. About one feminist in a hundred knows who she is, and she's one of the best poets in America. Or Grace Paley, who may be the best short story writer since Eudora Welty. Unknown. Unknown people because there's so much attention being put into this earthshoe consciousness: find out what's going on this year, be on top of it, so that you don't miss anything.

I Will Fight No More Forever—I haven't read it, I have no idea whether it's a good book or a bad book, but I know the consciousness that puts it on the library shelves. It comes from a certain pressure; it is not coming out of literature. It is coming from somebody saying, "Read some Indian stuff, read some women's stuff, read some black stuff." Just so that you'll have it down so you can look at all these guys and say, "Yeah, yeah, yeah; I've read all about wurchajig."

I looked through all of these books the high school kids are reading. They're not getting Faulkner; they're not getting Hemingway; they're not getting Melville; they're getting me. I'm not a classic; I'm not a wart on a classic's butt yet. I'm working at it, I may make it as a classic, but I know that I'm not in there with *Moby Dick* yet. You don't need to teach *Cuckoo's Nest;* there's nothing to be said about it. It teaches itself. It's a simple Christ allegory taking place in a nut house. Everybody can read it and plug in at their own level. The reason that it's taught is so that they can catch these kids' attention. When I go to a drugstore and I find Jack Nicholson on the cover of *Cuckoo's Nest,* I believe my "Yoknapatawpha County" is being subdivided by the land sharks and eventually they're going to be selling McMurphy-burgers down here on the corner. And that not only hurts me who was the creator of the work, but it hurts the person who is reading the work, because it's already polluted and becoming more and more polluted until—it's like the voices that are on the Saturday morning cartoons. People down there can't think of any new voices or new characters. All the voices are Ed Wynn, old voices, because they don't have the brains to think of anything new.

Always I'm reminded of French Peak up here. French Peak, for those who haven't kept track of it in the last ten years, is a place that they have been wanting to log so bad for so long that they don't really even want to log it anymore, they want to fight about it. There are no roads through it, no wires through it—it exists at an elevation, about an hour from Eugene here, that no other wilderness area exists at. At one argument we were having about the French Peak area, a logger stood up and said, "All those longhairs, these ecologists, and stuff like that, they never go up there. They're just talking about it like it's an abstract idea. We're loggers and we know the place. We want to get into it." (That's because it was a virgin, I think is what it was.) He says, "You're probably not even going to go up there this year." And I said, "That's probably right. I'm probably not going to go to the Library of Congress, either, but I don't want it logged."

I want it there forever; just like I want the Great Pyramid there forever so that I can go and look at it. "My God, look at that. There's that pyramid. I've seen it all my life on a pack of

Camels; it's there; it exists on the face of this earth; it belongs to me." It doesn't need to be obstructed on the skyline by this Japanese corporation that is moving in and building some kind of hotel the same shape as the pyramid right next to it. That's pollution.

I wish there were some good Buddhists in the country that would teach the Bible, instead of all these Christians. I mean, they're driving people away from the Bible by the droves. The Bible is, apart from anything God might've had to do with it, one hell of a book. People have forgotten this. It needs in some way to be taught. People are not going to learn it.

I went through a lengthy period of my life which I am going to go into now because it makes for a nice metaphor. Suddenly there were a bunch of us high and we realized that we had a chance to see the real books, the Karmic books. They weren't at the principal's office or down at the City Hall. These were the books that showed just where you stood in eternity, that showed how you were doing; if you were a gentle soul; if you were a harsh soul; if you were afraid; if you were courageous—it was right there. And we thought, "Hey, that's far out. Let's leave these other books alone and go to the real books."

So a lot of people did, for quite a long time, taking lots of stuff, breaking words apart, breaking sentences apart, breaking books apart. About twelve years ago, Kenneth Anger and Anton LaVey, the Crowleyite crew from San Francisco, were coming out to visit us at our house in La Honda. To make a point, I took all the books out of the house. All my good books I put over here and all the books I didn't want any part of I put over there and we were going to burn them, to make some kind of point. I have no idea what the point was, except that it was part of a chopping off of that old way. The guy whose job it was—his name was The Hermit—whose job it was to wheelbarrow the books up and put them in a great pile had got to the wrong pile of books, so he got all of my good books. I went up to the fire and there were all of my good books, but there was this audience already there and I was obligated to go ahead with the ritual, which included—this was on Mother's Day—

which included a hen that had been hoisted aloft in a golden cage in the branches of a redwood tree and a stump that had been sprayed gold and an axe in the stump, all of it sprayed gold. We let the hen down and there was an egg in the cage, I recall. The Hermit said, "Stomp that egg!" and I stomped egg. We chopped the head off the chicken, we plucked the chicken, we cleaned the chicken, burned the books, boiled the chicken. The chicken was just the awfulest thing you've ever tasted in your life—tasted just like burning books. My library, at that point, was no longer in existence. I thought, "Well, I've already burned all my good books; I might as well burn all my bad books." I wheeled them up there and then burned them. I have kicked myself around the block for this a dozen times.

It wasn't too many years after that in my quest to look at the real books, that it was as though a big hand grabbed me by the back of the neck and says, "YOU WANT TO SEE THE REAL BOOKS, HUH?" and forced me, nose to the page, to look for about thirty hours at the inequities of mankind, at every ungentle act and lie and coercion that I had ever done. Finally after seeing all the things that were wrong with myself, going on through the Vietnamese war and finally right out to everybody starving everywhere, I realized that is the real books. And it's what hell is, for hour after hour after hour to see where you really are and what the situation of the world really is. It scared the pants off of me.

This happened in about 1968 or '69. I'd been in England briefly before this and was impressed with the way the children spoke, in England. They spoke a whole lot better than us Oregonians, let me tell you. In England I began to get a sense of something that I had lost. I didn't know that it was lost; all I knew was there was an emptiness, and it had been for some years.

Here's the way I feel that these drugs affected us. They cut off our periphery time sense, so here we just were, floating. Our minds were scattered. We weren't worrying about where we were going or where we had been. After a length of time of this, we wanted to go somewhere. We saw that there is a light ahead;

there are things to be done, in each community and in each heart. So we started trying to make it toward this light, but we couldn't steer the boat. We had turned loose the tiller; the boat was awash in the sea. When you're lost in superstition and dope, you're lost. A lot of people were.

I believe we're competing with "Sesame Street" and "Welcome Back, Kotter" on a whole lot bigger level than anybody understands. I believe you've got to reach out there and get these kids right by their noses. This isn't supposed to be a psychodrama that I'm sending my kids to. I'll do that at home; I'll take care of their psyches at home; I will be their counselor and guru at home. I send these kids to school because I want them to sit down, shut up, open up their book, and learn how to read.

Here's the way to do it. Right now I could take a bunch of these kids that I know in Pleasant Hill because I work with them—they're the wrestlers, they're the football players. I know these guys. They're smart. They're being dumb because it's hip. If I had *Moby Dick* to work with in a class of twenty-five or thirty kids that I was bigger than, I could say, "Okay, we're starting on *Moby Dick*. Open it to page one. You! Stand up and read." He has to stand up and read: "Call me Ishmael." He reads until somebody over there giggles at a mistake in a word. "Okay. You! Stand up and read." And you don't let them get away; you don't let that mind loose until the end of that hour. That's the way that "Sesame Street" is playing it and if we're going to fight, that's the way we're going to have to fight them. We're going to have to reach back in there and grapple for the minds of our children. And it's going to take people that love books and love literature enough to join in this fight because the teachers can't handle it themselves. We've let it slip too long.

My short story teacher at the University of Oregon was a guy named J. B. Hall. He was a controversial character there because he wore white shoes. At that time, wearing white shoes meant that you were either a faggot or a commie, or maybe both. Anyway, he at one time pointed out to me a part in a short story called "Soldier's Home" by Hemingway in which this guy Krebs has come home from the war and he's sitting there in the morning wondering what to do with the day—whether to go watch his sister play indoor baseball or just exactly what. His mother wants him to go get a job, but he doesn't want to move. As he's sitting there, he watches the bacon fat harden on his plate. And J. B. Hall says, "See, that's what it is. There's where it happens; right there." And I saw it. I saw, "Right! That's what it's about! That's what literature is about!" And a door opened up to me and it's never been closed. I thank this man from the bottom of my heart. It's a turn-on like—it has nothing to do with intelligence. It has to do with somebody grabbing somebody and saying:

"I know something that's good. I'll give it to you for nothing. You'll have it all your life."

The challenge of literature today for the writer is not to write about the dogshit on the streets in New York, but write about how somebody rises above the dogshit on the streets of New York. It has become so popular to write about the anti-hero living in the dogshit, in fact glorifying in the dogshit. There are a couple of girls at Pleasant Hill that are freshmen; I've known them for a long time. They're headed for doom. They have gone out two or three times—bought a couple of bottles of Mad Dog 20–20, fallen down, broken their teeth, broken their glasses. They've had two or three motorcycle wrecks. They have run away from home. Everybody knows the syndrome. What's wrong with them? They don't have any sense of the eternal. Where are they going to get it? They're not going to church. There's no church for them. Even if they go, their ears can't hear it. They can't find their place anymore. And yet they're screaming with their mouths bleeding and laying in the dust of the motorcycle. They're screaming for some direction.

We've had warriors fighting in this arena for a long, long time. They have left us a lot of records of how to fight. Martin Buber's *I and Thou* is as strong a book as I know to teach somebody about how to live in this world and relate to the world and relate to God at the same time, so that you don't become one-sided like George Wallace who chops off part of himself and becomes strong but one side of himself is gone.

Patty Hearst is the metaphor for these girls. She's like a blackboard; anything can write on her. What is going to write on her if we don't? If somebody doesn't step in and take up the chalk and write words of Shakespeare or Yeats on this blackboard, what is going to be written on it is going to be pornography, is going to be shallow stuff, pap at its worst level because it caters to these particular lost girls and it leads them further and further into lostness instead of leading them toward any light.

Everybody in this room has pretty much the same idea that I have about what the light is. One time somebody was saying, "But you're so much more enlightened than I am." Paul Foster was sitting nearby and says, "The light is seven million miles away and we're all clustered up back here at 5 inches, 5½ inches, 6 inches, 6½ inches." Maybe somebody's a half an inch ahead of somebody, but that's about all. When it comes to really going toward the light, the people in this room are about as enlightened as it gets. I know Baba Ram Dass, I know Tim Leary, I know all the honchos of enlightenment. There isn't a one of them that knows anything that everybody in this room doesn't know. It's time we fought for it. It's time we fought when we say, "*Moby Dick* is better than *The Carpetbaggers*. Okay? *Moby Dick* is better than *The Carpetbaggers*. The Taj Mahal is better than the Holiday Inn. The Eugene Armory is better than the Federal Building."

*John Perry Barlow is a Grateful Dead lyricist, investiga-
tive journalist, former rancher, and "anti-company guy"
with a special interest in issues having to do with com-
munications technology.*

EULOGY FOR KEN

By John Perry Barlow

Kesey. You are still a trip. And I will always be on it.

What a man you were. And do I mean man. What a bull, all
beef and energy and power, and sometimes, wild craziness. The
meat is now discarded. The power and the energy—and certainly the wild craziness—still snort through our consciousness, which you did so much to expand.

I don't grieve for you. You knew long before I did that there
are meadows for the soul. Jed led you to them. Now you're
there with him and your grief is over. I'm sorry for us, but because I know how little truck you had with self-pity, I'm trying
not to be too sorry for us.

Still. I will miss your magnificent bullshit. I will miss the little Prankster smile at the corners of your mouth. I will miss
your mythic stories and the life you led that was so rich in their
production. I will miss the lean clarity of your words. No one of
your generation wrote better than you.

I will miss your nearly concealed sweetness of heart, the
softness that stirred beneath the muscle, the disappearing
bunny of your soul. I will even miss your faults, the weaknesses
that almost rendered you human scale.

You were the last Titan of my Bohemian life. The latest crop of us seem soft on the outside and hard within. There are no more Cassadys or Kerouacs. There is no more Kesey.

I wish I could be there to watch them plant you out in your garden. But I am in the Belly of the Beast today, Washington, D.C., putting in a lonely word for freedom. You never gave an inch in its service, and I will live for it as you would have me do.

Maybe one day I'll be able to identify all the qualities that grew into me from you. I know that you became part of me, just as Neal lived on in you. But right now, you are too generally distributed in my psyche to sort out into anything but gratitude.

So. Thank you, Ken. Thank you for everything. Thank you for myself.

Love,
Barlow

James Baker Hall is a poet, novelist, photographer, and teacher. He was Poet Laureate of Kentucky, 2001–03.

KEN

By James Baker Hall

The only time I was around Ken the person in any ongoing way, I was at his elbow as he read *One Flew Over the Cuckoo's Nest*, a chapter at a time, to the advanced fiction workshop at Stanford in the school year 1960–61, a group of twelve or so gathered to an oval around a big modern Danish table, mostly fellowship-holding full-time writers, some with published books. We met in the Jones Room, the writing program's private digs elevator-high up in the library, with its own honor-system collection of modern fiction and poetry, many of the books still in their dust jackets, its own setup for coffee and tea and lounging, long before writing programs were commonplace. Iowa was the only other program of note, and it wasn't being underwritten by Bay Area "rich heels," as Theodore Roethke called them. Next to the library, sharing the Jones Room's space in the grand scope of things, was the Hoover Tower, Hoo Tow, a conservative think-tank before conservative think-thanks were named. Beneath us, in the large main reading room on the second floor of the library, at the same station almost every day, known perhaps to a few of the students in his purview, sat the eighty-year-old Aleksandr Feodorovich Kerensky with his books gathered around him, the Premier of 1917 Russia, in the hot seat when the Bolsheviks staged the takeover. Hardly Big Nurse, the spirit surrounding the Jones Room at Stanford at the end of the '50s, but hardly City Lights Bookstore up the freeway in San Francisco's North Beach either, where Ginsberg, Corso, and Kerouac were being published, and where Ken and *Cuckoo's Nest* would have fit right in.

When he read—and sometimes when he listened—Ken propped his knees up on the edge of the table and leaned himself and his chair back on two legs, the cuffs of his jeans folding back over his thick sockless ankles onto his football calves. When he finished a page he had to lean forward in his tight t-shirt, reaching out to put it facedown on the table, and you could see how native he was to his body, and how powerful-looking, with a neck like the bole of an oak tree. The ball player and wrestling champion in Ken I felt a kinship with, as an ex-jock myself, and we were both prematurely balding, too, itself a serious though voiceless bond, but the drug-head and wild man in him scared me, and as for the work, well, others were more impressed with it than I was as it was coming down. I remember trying to convince him that his language had to be absolutely clear on what was real in his story, and what was fantasy—he listened, more out of camaraderie than interest in what I had to say. If he thought my mind needed expanding, he was right. He went home to fun, I to dread of WWIII. A constipated screech owl, someone called me in my twenties, newly bookish with big horn-rims.

The first quarter we had the good fortune of Malcolm Cowley in his early sixties at the head of the table, with his hearing aid turned on, with his beautiful New England tweedy manners foremost. Cowley had written a widely read book about the Lost Generation, he'd recovered Faulkner from out-of-print obscurity and seen him through the Nobel Prize, he'd known Hemingway, Fitzgerald, Hart Crane, Dos Passos. We felt like we were in literary history, listening to most anything he had to say. As a powerful consultant for Viking, as someone who'd been in on the publication of *On the Road*, Cowley's excitement about what Ken was reading to us, and the contract implicit in that excitement, gave the emerging novel special status, but I don't remember anyone knowing it would be the book we'd be talking about forty years later. Larry McMurtry was reading chapters of *Leaving Cheyenne*, those mesmerizing dialogues between Gid and Johnny, both in love with Molly: that would have been my nominee for the keeper among us.

Ken was an orderly on a psych ward, and a guinea pig for drug doctors. He sneaked nameless pills out of the hospital in the cuffs of his jeans; he passed them around, if he liked you and thought you needed goosing. He messed with the doctors at work, too, misreporting his experiences in their experiments. Perry Lane, where he was the major-domo, had carried the flag of bohemianism all the way back to Thorstein Veblen in the '20s. Some of the essays in *Our Changing Order* were written on Perry Lane, where Ken and his supporting cast were unfolding a new revolution. The Cold War was in the not-too-distant background, Elvis was in the air, Ike was campaigning for Nixon. I wasn't the only one who found Ken's life more compelling than his work—already it was theatrical, larger than other lives, freer, fuller-seeming, more surprising and nervy and energetic and real, more shameless and inventive, even as it seemed cartoonish and too often irresponsible. Some thought that Ken and the Perry Lane culture were a menace to civilization, Wallace Stegner among them, the writing program's famous director. A bunch of Stanford fraternity boys showed up at Ken's one night, to crash a party maybe, for sure to cause trouble, and Ken threw the leader into the bushes—shazam!—on his speedy way to becoming a counterculture hero, and turning his life into a work of art-in-progress, a meaty finger raised to Wally Stegner and the rich heels. Manhood may have been Kesey's deepest theme, I find myself thinking now—even the great cause of individual freedom served it, did it not; and theatricality his truest style. Music delivered Elvis to his groin, frontier history delivered Ken to his. He had to jump higher, dive deeper, and stay under longer than any man alive, the glorious lineage of Mike Fink and the Red River Roarers. His song was the boast, his story's hero its designated singer. *Cuckoo* was calling his own bluff, having to get McMurphy on up to the brag.

For the winter and spring quarter Cowley was replaced by

an elegantly fiery Irishman in his late fifties named Michael O'Donovan who called himself Frank O'Connor, thought by many to be one of the great masters of the short story form. He'd known Joyce and Yeats, he'd been the Director of the Abbey Theater, a specialist when it came to telling a real shazam from a make-believe. Week after week for six months one after another of us read what we thought were short stories: Peter Beagle, Larry, Gurney Norman, Joanna Ostrow, Judith Rascoe, Ken, the Australian Chris Koch, a very classy bunch of young writers, and the master kept telling us we didn't know what a short story was. Only two of our efforts so much as qualified, and neither was what he would call a masterpiece, he'd been sent to tell us. With his grand white hair and roguish good looks, Mr. O'Connor kept himself at a patrician distance from the big table at the head there, and turned away, not exactly listening over his rumpled shoulder, but with suspicion you might have to notice, staring off into the knowing distance, a pipe sticking up out of the handkerchief pocket of his seersucker jacket, his fingertip-to-tip hands somewhere in the picture. Everything about this man was beautiful and charming, even if he didn't like *Cuckoo's Nest*, and several of us thought that his young American wife from Annapolis had distinguished herself and her country, and that their three-year-old daughter was an enchanted creature, even if he and Ken were chips on each other's shoulder. The discussions that followed on the short-story readings, Mr. O'Connor would tolerate for as long as he could stand it that day, and then break in to inform us, "It's *not* a story!" bringing the whole of Irish patriarchy to bear on the pronunciation of *sto*-rry.

"Why not?" Ken was soon to challenge him.

"It doesn't bend the barr!"

The Oregon lumberjack in Ken or the division-one wrestler might have understood what Mr. O'Connor meant by that better than the rest of us, being less a sucker for concepts, but he wouldn't tolerate being looked down upon. Or was it, already, couldn't stand not being looked up to? At some point, Ken quit coming to the O'Connor workshop. In a reminiscence called

"Ken at Stanford," Cowley reports that Ken tried, with at least some success, to get others of us to join his rebellion, à la Mc-Murphy in *Cuckoo's Nest.* That sounds like something one would remember, which I don't, and it sounds like a lot of trouble for a group I remember as having very little, just the opposite in fact. We loved what we had going there in the Jones Room—if Ken couldn't get along with Mr. O'Connor, he was the only one.

At the going-away party for Cowley at Ken's place, there was dry ice in the green punch, double double toil and trouble, and who knows what else. I didn't go to sleep for two days. I remember sitting next to him against a wall in the living room, our knees up, and watching the people in the room crowd and uncrowd themselves. Across the way in the kitchen was Mr. Cowley, in a tie-less sports jacket and button-down blue broadcloth shirt, hitting on Ken's grandmother's moonshine from Arkansas, thanks to whoever told him to avoid the punch. Someone directed his attention to us, Ken and I were smiling and waving encouragement. He smiled and waved back, with a hearing-aid-less look on his kind face—then returned to Ken's granny and her contribution to the festivities. At some juncture of our companionship that night, I noticed that Ken looked like a Van Gogh, with his wavy blond hair receding, his blue eyes keen, bright, that portrait of . . . just as well I can't pin it down, for it's only a surface resemblance. It lacks Ken's mischief, and scariness. We were sitting against another wall, cross-legged this time. He took off his tall hat, upsidedowning it at his side, and turned down his cuff, offering me whatever was in there—white ones, blue ones, purple, green, yellow. My twenty-five-year-old heart leapt and thumped, I had to go deep to breathe. Someday I'd have to swallow something like that, I knew that, but not now, not me, not now.

No thanks, I signaled.

Are you sure, he signaled back—donning the Uncle Sam's hat.

"I'm sure," I told him. Not me, not now.

He cornered people and scared them, not so many as Elvis and Mick, but in the same Dionysian way. Kesey had a flair-become-genius for jumping the traces, cutting loose, letting the Id into play—he got off on it, it was his subvocal transmission, his guiding spirit. As *Cuckoo's Nest* testifies, I think, being the bullgoose loonie was his money shot, his deepest knowledge. If you were adventuresome, and on the ready, he could goose you good—if you weren't, your tight ass got tighter. The Hell's Angels were in the offing, you just knew it, a gang bang with the woman's scary husband present—which one were you, where could you hide? Whatever you were afraid of, it was wired into him, the guy in the tall striped hat who could really work a crowd, large or small—Mr. Stegner had good reason to feel menaced.

I wish *tribe* hadn't become such a trendy word, because it's the exact right one for what was going on every which way I turned throughout the '60s: Tribes were forming and unforming, some digging in, others free-form to urban life, appearing only to disappear and reappear. The Merry Pranksters were the best known of the Perry Lane tribes, but not the only one, and there was a Jones Room tribe, for lifelong friendships were formed at Stanford. There was a Kentucky tribe that intermingled out West for years, before returning home, one and then another. Not families, not communities, but tribes, shaped by myths and open horizons, blood mingled at the wrists that would dry and flake but never disappear. After that year at Stanford, I saw Ken in the flesh here and there from time to time, in New York and Kentucky mostly but never for more than a few minutes, at the same time that I was never far from Ken writ large, known to most as Kesey, or that time with our backs to the wall when Van Gogh was in him, and he showed me the dangerous, colorful pills. There was an ingrained sweetness about the man, a lovableness, cut straight across the grain with his will to power: a bluntness in his heart-shaped joker face, a narrowing, for good or ill, most apparent when he scared you.

The great folk/blues artist and storyteller Rosalie Sor-
rels was a valued friend of Kesey's for many years. She
lives near Boise, Idaho, in a cabin built by her father,
and continues to tour, perform, and record regularly.
The song "My Last Go Round" can be heard on her 2000
collection Borderline Heart.

LAST GO ROUND:

A Song for Ken Kesey

By Rosalie Sorrels

Photo by William Campbell

It was a great party . . . celebrating the advent of *Sailor Song* at
the Kesey spread. He had a spot he called "the swamp" (looked
more like a clearing in the forest to me) where he'd built a stage

that looked like a ship and since the story takes place in Alaska, there were large representations of those beautiful red and black on white animal spirit pictures . . . the bear . . . the raven . . . the owl . . . flying in the trees like great kites. It looked like about a thousand (mostly young) people were there. I think a lot of them thought they were going to see the Grateful Dead . . . and that might have happened but Jerry wasn't feeling too great and couldn't make it. Robert Hunter made it, though, and he wrote a lot of those songs . . . and Rambling Jack Elliott was there and I was there. Anne Waldman came and read poetry . . . she was awesome (as the children say) . . . and Ken went out and got all the good musicians who live around Eugene. You can find good musicians anywhere if you're paying attention, and no one ever paid attention better than Ken Kesey. They played on that ship of dreams all day, old songs . . . new songs . . . blues . . . old timey music . . . everything you could want to hear. What a party!

When it began to be twilight, the stage was set up for something else . . . a fire pit appeared . . . with a fire. On close inspection, the stone fire ring was drawn on paper and contained a color wheel and a fan blowing cellophane strings in the red light . . . but close inspection spoils the magic and none of us were into that. There was a huge screen set up so images could be projected, and out stepped Ken Kesey in a flowing robe and a double storytelling mask. Standing with his back to us, he was first the Raven . . . announcing the story of the *Sea Lion*, which is contained in *Sailor Song* and also published separately as a children's book with beautiful illustrations. Turning slowly, he became the Old Woman and told the old tale of the changeling . . . the creature who is a man upon the land . . . a sea lion in the sea. While he spoke the images from the book were projected on the screen and he was joined by several children who played the sea monsters . . . pure magic. At the end all those young people rose and cheered as though they had in fact been to a rock and roll concert and I thought . . . Huzzah . . . the attention span has returned!

Later, after the swamp had been cleared and everyone had

gone home or to the next place, following the light of giant luminarias made from translucent soy milk containers, several of us sat around the big round table in the Kesey kitchen and, over one of the better bourbons I have ever tasted, Ken told me about his next book about the first roundup at Pendleton, Oregon, in 1911: *Last Go Round.* I grew up around rodeo people and that phrase rattled my memory cage, reminding me that at a rodeo it means the last, best, hardest ride when all the amateurs have gone and only the pros are left . . . in my family, it meant the last, best, hardest work you do . . . if that is dying, you'd want to do it right.

The song came sweetly and easily . . . the first and last verses and the tune almost all together, and I began to sing it a lot, but I never felt like it was finished. Everyone liked it and they often sang along. Finally I got to Eugene and called Ken to see if I could come over and sing it to him. Next thing I knew I was doing just that, and when I had finished he said, "That's really pretty, but it's not finished . . . it's a rodeo story . . . you need a rodeo verse." The book hadn't been published yet, but he handed me the uncorrected proof and said, "Now you read this . . . find a line you like . . . steal it and write a rodeo verse." So I must admit that the second verse was shamelessly stolen from the last line of the first chapter (page 8), and the rest of the verse reflects my vast admiration for one of the best western writers I ever read . . . the rest of the song reflects my great affection for one of the best human beings I've had the good fortune to know.

What a party

What a party

What a party!!!

Last Go Round

Words & Music by Rosalie Sorrels

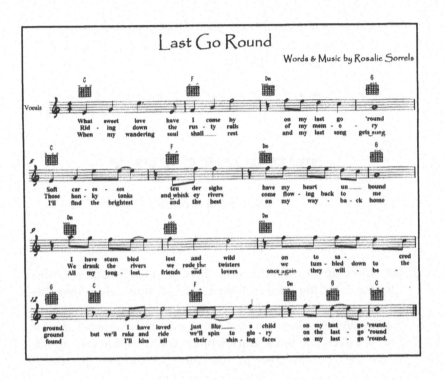

What sweet love have I come by on my last go 'round
Rid - ing down the rus - ty rails of my mem - o - ry
When my wandering soul shall rest and my last song gets sung

Soft car - es - ses ten - der sighs have my heart un - bound
Those hon - ky tonks and whisk - ey rivers come flow - ing back to me
I'll find the brightest and the best on my way - ba - ck home

I have stum - bled lost and wild on to sa - cred the
We drank the rivers we rode the twisters we tum - bled down to
All my long - lost friends and lovers once again they will - be -

ground. I have loved just like a child on my last go 'round.
ground but we'll rake and ride we'll spin to glo - ry on the last - go 'round.
found I'll kiss all their shin - ing faces on my last - go 'round.

ROSALIE SORRELS "My Last Go Round"

157

Eileen Babbs teaches high school English in Eugene, and is married to Kesey's lifelong friend and partner Ken Babbs. They live in Dexter.

THE WHITE TENT

By Eileen Babbs

We drove up to the farm and there it stood—majestic, taut, glowing from the lantern light inside—a huge white tent. We could see a few dark figures silhouetted against the sides. Babbs said it looked like something out of Afghanistan. And it did. It looked like those stark white structures that rise up out of the barren landscapes in that country we were bombing the crap out of—on the periphery of our grief.

Kesey had died a few nights before, and we were making nightly visits to his home, "the farm." I spent the days baking things to bring and answering the incessant phone: *People* magazine, a reporter from AP, *Rolling Stone*, wanting to be assured a seat at the memorial, the local paper. (Babbs wouldn't talk to any of them. He wrote a statement for me to read to them, a trick he said he learned from Kesey after Leary died.)

At night we went to the farm. We were digging the grave. Just as they had dug Kesey's son Jed's grave, but someone mentioned that Jed had had many able-bodied frat brothers, who got the job done fairly quickly. We were moving more at Prankster pace. Someone would jump in the hole, dig for a while—not somber as you might expect, just gentle conversation, passing a bottle, sipping on a beer. People would wander out from the house, bring a few beers.

I liked the look of the tent best from the distance of the

kitchen. Like something biblical rising out of the mist. The kids—Kesey's grandchildren, his brother's grandchildren, and other children who were family of sorts—stayed out there, leaping in and out of the hole, playing in the mound of dirt that was steadily getting higher.

The tent had appeared on the second or third night. They had attempted to erect another, flimsier structure the first night. Blue. The phone rang the next morning. It was Faye. The blue tent had collapsed. "Ha!" yelled my daughter from her bed. "I knew it! You should have seen them putting that up. They had like eight pieces left when they were done."

It threatened rain all week. The winds would kick up like they do before a rain. But it still hadn't rained. We were worried the grave would turn into a muddy mess. Faye wasn't sure who had ordered the white tent. But it was handsome. And didn't flinch a bit in the wind.

The hole itself was a perfect rectangle. No roots. No rock. No clay. Just good stiff Oregon dirt. It didn't crumble down the sides like you'd expect, and the angles were quite square.

I jumped down in the hole one of those nights and dug a few shovelfuls. Big tears plopped down on the dirt.

As the hole got deeper they had to lower a ladder to get the diggers out. It was getting there. Once in a while someone would ask a digger, "How tall are you?" And it was thus that we gauged the depth.

Babbs, Liz, and I drove over to the farm the morning of the memorial service. It was eerily warm, but still no rain. I grabbed a copy of a poem that I'd heard Kesey recite, and Babbs read it to Liz in the car: "I went out to the hazel wood/ Because a fire was in my head . . ."

The plan was to ride the bus in to Eugene. When we got to the farm, the tent was empty; Faye was in the house wondering aloud whether to wear her hair up or down. Down, we decided. She looked girlish but with her eternal calm. George drove the bus. Babbs and Faye in their usual seats. Faye sitting straight-backed, as she would throughout the day. As my sister had sat at her son's funeral, ramrod straight.

Kesey's seat behind the driver, too damn empty. Babbs kind of slid halfway over, picking out the sounds. He sat hunched over the CDs and the CD player. "On the Road Again."

"The life I love is makin' music with my friends . . ."

I looked at Stephanie, Zane's wife, and our tears ran down in little rivers.

We stumbled into the packed theater. Kind of dark and confusing. The first person to stand up and greet us looked familiar. Good-looking guy. (Damn! I think this is Bob Weir, but I'm not sure!) I turned and said, "This is Liz, our daughter." (I found out later that it was Bob Weir.)

Dave Frohnmayer, the president of the University of Oregon, spoke first. It was an incredible speech—humorous, nostalgic, perfect transitions, polished and eloquent, all nicely bound in a leather notebook.

Babbs's speech is on little scraps of paper stuffed in different pockets. For the past week I have been watching him whip these out to make his notes at inspired moments. I shift in my seat, fretting. What the hell is it going to sound like after Frohnmayer's speech? Silly question. He leapt onto the stage, after realizing there was no other way up. Smacked his hand on Kesey's coffin. Pulled the scraps of paper out of his pocket. And did his thing.

His Prankster thing. His Babbs thing. His funny, sad, humble, poetic thing, forgetting details and facts, but never forgetting his mission. His voice finally caught at the end as he described a flock of birds swooping up out of the fog at the farm on the morning of Kesey's death. And I understood why he had refused to speak to any reporters.

This friendship was epic, and I suddenly felt very small.

We caught a ride back to the farm. Faye wanted Kesey to ride the bus back alone. Still no rain. It was cloudy, but the clouds were high and the air was oddly sultry. The white tent was transformed, full of flowers, tall, pungent showy flowers, and there was AstroTurf, folding chairs, a stand for the coffin.

Kesey's cousin spoke first, about growing up with Ken. He was our leader, he said. When we were children he always had the plan, the best ideas. Like the time they filled a shed full of cattail fluff. And Kesey dove in from the rafters. Yep, we all nodded. He had the goofiest ideas sometimes.

Liz wanted me to read the Yeats poem "The Song of the Wandering Aengus," but I was too chicken. She did it. Loud and clear and sweet and youthful: "The silver apples of the moon,/The golden apples of the sun."

We all filed past the coffin. "Put something in if you want," Zane said. I had nothing but a ring that a friend, Kathy, had given me. So I took that off and put it in. People had put in notes and flowers, and I could see joints poking out of his pockets, for the road. I walked past Faye and it seemed like she was frowning at me, but I couldn't understand why.

Babbs told me the next day that he was behind me, fishing around Kesey's feet! He thought I'd tossed our wedding ring in there. Faye probably thought he was up to his old shenanigans. Grabbing a joint for himself or something.

As I drove home alone that night down the back-country road, the local radio station was playing the Grateful Dead, a live show. Then a voice, slightly hysterical. It was Kesey! Talking about Bill Graham's death and his son's death. About the Dead reaching out to him in his grief and Bill Graham paying for the pedestal in Jed's memory on Mt. Pisgah. He recited the e.e. cummings poem "Buffalo Bill's Defunct":

> . . . *how do you like your blueeyed boy*
> *Mister Death*

He screamed it and I wanted to scream along with him, barreling down the dark back road from Kesey's house.

———

The next day, Babbs was meeting the guys at the Pleasant Hill pizza place. Feeling aimless and unfinished, I drove back over to the farm. The tent was gone and Faye's brother was out there sweeping up the AstroTurf carpet. I helped him sweep it and roll it up. As we got to the last roll it finally started to rain . . . soft, warm, Oregon autumn rain.

Jim Dodge teaches at Humboldt State University and is the author of three novels and several volumes of poetry. His latest book is Rain on the River, *a collection of new and selected poetry and prose.*

A CEREMONY OF CONSOLATION

By Jim Dodge

Kesey, whenever I'm explaining the difference
between "farther" and "further" to another class,
between distances you can measure with a ruler
and those only the soul can calibrate,
I'll remember you on the converted bus,
the destination placard declaring "Further,"
Cassady at the wheel,
and I'll recall your star-spangled, All-American,
pure-product-gone-crazy grin,
the life and mischief in your eyes,
and I'll say to myself
what Chief Bromden in Cuckoo's Nest,
who has a fondness for chewing gum,
says to McMurphy—
this after 20 years of being ostensibly mute—
when McMurphy, in the simplest gesture of kindness,
slips the Chief a stick of Juicy Fruit:
"Thank you."

Kesey and Gurney Norman became friends in the 1960–61 writing class at Stanford. Norman's landmark novel of the 1960s, Divine Right's Trip, *originally appeared in* The Last Whole Earth Catalog. *He has taught for many years at the University of Kentucky.*

A CORRESPONDENCE

By Ken Kesey and Gurney Norman

Pleasant Hill, OR
March 16, 1986

Gurney Norman
Lexington, Kaintook

Dear Gurn:

St. Paddy's Eve . . . Faye and I just home a few days from our lit bit Down Under . . . finally dug and dusted my way back into my cobwebbed computor. Things in pretty good shape, considering. Worst news was old Johnny died the day we got back. Forty-one years old. In horse years that's 41. Best news is that my galleys are going at last to print (after torturous weeks of me correcting New York's incorrections) and Chuck says the book is finally sparking some tentative east-coast enthusiasm.

How's Wilgus and the folks? Hear tell there's a lot of lay-offs back yonder, surely hope they weren't effected. Honest work's tough to come by, these days. And the rest of the old gang? I suspect they must be fine else I'd have heard otherwise. Things are beginning to spring about around here. Eight baby calves, the eighth only an afternoon old. And the army of daffodils Faye planted last fall are on the march along our drive like a hoard of gaudy Mongols.

Australia? Why, mate, try one of <u>these</u>, they'll give you a taste. Passionfruit lollies we brought back. Purple, matches my eye. Aint that some exotic taste? Shirley brought a sack by our hotel fresh from her mum's tree every morn. I would spoon out the seeds and mix them with rum in my red bottle, plus mango and papaya and guelibbleah and all those other exotic juices. Some ice and shake, crushes all those flavors together. Passion punch by the bunch Bob Stone and I slugged down those last two weeks. It's the hot of summer down there right now yer know; one-bloody-hundred-and-fifteen it got one afternoon in Adelaide. So ya can see how a digger needs liquids down yonderly, steady and palatable and prefferably with spirit inhancement. <u>Lots</u> of liquids.

Consequently, when we got back the other day I brought home with me—along with a 400 (Australian) dollar didjerido and a 30 hour jet lag—a two week backlog of hangover. Not to mention my what? Ah, right; my passion purple blue-ribbon-of-a-shiner? Well, it's a bit of a story, it is, but I knowd some blokes were bound to pry, soon or late. Just let me sketch a few quick impressions, first, to work into the mood . . .

Feb, twenty-four, eighty-six, hip! In the air
On our way

Down to San Fran then to L.A.
Then to Adelaide, Australia—
Faye and I
And all our parphenalia.

Reading Tropic of Cancer, first few pages,
Reviewing bygone bohemian messages—
Which said to our young Yankee heart, in part:

Go to Paris.
Study art.
Get dirty.
Get smart.

A fine old marching lyric, late of the Lost
Generation Company, Paris Platoon. A noble outfit, now defunct. Wiped out after the disasterous
Abstract Expressionism ambush and the skyrocket-
ing rent rates for studio space on the Left Bank.
Saw action in most of the many Dirty Book Bat-
tles and brought glory to their company during
the historic Cubist Confrontation, fighting and
painting tirelessly without rulers or rules.
Great revolutionaries from a glorious revolution, mainly lost, mostly defunct. But we can make
out the echoing fragments of that cultural clash,
though it's fifty years finished or so. Like lines
spelt in smoke, words wafted assunder. Then,
sometimes, when you're reading Henry Miller and
drinking Bordouix wine, let's say, or listening
to a Cole Porter song, or wandering along a sun-
swept beach and see on the monochrome sand an
arrangement of gullshit and driftwood and are
reminded of a painting by George Braque . . . these
smokey song snatches might waft up, and drift near
and wind together again long enough for the wan-
derer to piece out a kind of hazy semper fidelis.

Words for long-ago losers to live by. A credo, for such wild and wooly young skates from the States as longed to try their wheels on a different rink, to a different tune.

In its fullvoiced heyday this credo must have been just the impetus needed to prick a lot of skinny, hungry, artsyfartsy sorts free of their shilly-shally shuffling round and round the slow-rolling circle of conventional society. Pick up speed! Fast and fly, and lie where you light, among foreigners and fleas and the sweet reek of neurons a-snapping. Wipe the scales from your left eye with hand from Gauguin, off the right with Van Gogh's Starry Night. Leaven your loaf with the wordyeast of Yeats. Tattoo your private and tenderest skin——"PARIS TIMES DIRT EQUALS ART"——with the loan of a pin from Anais Nin.

All very sharp, very go-go stuff, in the go-stick twenties and thirties. In the eighties? Even Go has gone blunt. The go-stick doesn't even give a good starting prick. Which is just as well. Get our lad ground to mush before he got so much as a lap most like, let alone get up to escape velocity. Today's round-and-rounds are as remorselessly fast as yesterday's were slow. Modern technology, rack-and-pinion roller mounts. Skate of the art. Nowadays, there's no leeways for the shilly-shally shuffle out-of-phase, not with the kind of pace being set by these gnarly new muscle-mouthed ball-bearing eighteen-roller Rambo models rumbling around. Go to Paris? Not when Paris is included as part of the Holyland tour packages and art is something that's supposed to be left undisturbed, like a well-fed baby, sweet and luminescent during nap not to mention peaceful. Get smart? Not with all these legions of slobbery great

mumblebound Rambo lips alla time coming atcha with
what the credo of _our_ day is, mumbling subhumal re-
minders from every main gut and gutteral and good
ol boy gruntwork with a boobtube above the bar—
that it's not only unna-_cool_ to be too smart,
it's also unna-'_Murrikin_! Not when dirt is the
obscene rise of the teen-age suicide rate, the
Ausie kids now neck and neck with the other glo-
bal front-runners—Japan and Germany and the
U.S.A. . . . the only thing snuffing out more of
these bright young flames in these far flung na-
tions being alcohol-related car accidents, a suicide of sorts, themselves. I mean, what do you
tell 700 highschool kids bussed from all over Adelaide to hear the famous wiseman Guru Gung Ho? Go
to Paris? Study art? Not bleedin likely. Get
dirty? They are _all_ exceeding well-scrubbed and
primped-out in their lovely school unies, each
bunched together about the shadey places in their
school colors—pleats and plaid over there from
Christchurch Tech, khaki shirts and shorts there
from General Montgomery Military, over there the
fleet from Admiral Nelsen Academy in gleaming
white and navy with matching blue bowties for the
pink-cheeked lads or pert blue hankies in the
budding blouse pockets of the bright-eyed lasses.
So I might could tell 'em Go get dirty, as a possible wiseman suggestion, except what would I
tell their slovenly American counterpart in, say,
Pittsburg, Penn? Go wash up?

All I could think was give them the straight
party line: "There's good stuff and there's bad
stuff, free market democracy be damned! The bad
stuff rots. It don't make no difference how many
people vote for it, or read it, or drum it up
till a nothing tune can become a solid gold million album hummer—it still rots. And a lot of

those humdrumillions rot right along with it. They've invested too much or they've ingested too much. It turns to dross and drags them under.

"Good stuff, on the other hand, rises. It lives and it lifts. Lasts. That's the reason so much of it appears so drab and wave-worn—been bobbing around there on the briny for bloody centuries. Tiresome chunks of leftover flotsem—dullish worn. But should you ever find yourself in the gloomy soup, mates, a-sea alone, washed over and going under, latch hard to any of that dull old stuff bobbing by Bach . . . Blake . . . Beethoven . . . Michelangelo . . . _Shake_speare!—and see if they don't bouy a poor sinkin soul up yet a few waves longer. Verily I sez unto yer, mates and mate-resses, they can be located amidst the roaringest tempest, these reliable old livesavers . . . and latched onto from out the most reef-ripped tumult of insubstantial wreckage. They are called The Classics. Any mediocre teacher ought to know what they are, these Classics. A good teacher can teach you how to pick the floaters out of the tumult of sinkers. A great teacher makes the thing yours, for keeps, tucked down in your survival kit at the ready, like aspirin, or adrenaline, or your best friend's phone number.

"So, lastly, young Sheilas and Bills, verily I saz unto you all: give listen to your teachers when they sounds on about these antique flotsems what are e-clapt Classics never mind if it listens dull. And never mind whether they be great teachers, or mediocre, or as dull-seeming, say, as some old beer-bottle bobbing in the trashline out the bay, too bleached and battered to reveal at first the note rolled up within. The message, that is the thing of it, if you can get it rolled out and read—the message, not the bottle.

"But above all never mind all these popular detractors who, like Pink Floyd, keep chanting at you about not needing no education. "It's stupid to study," is the lesson these treacherous types all teach, "and it's smart to be dumb." They are this season's version of Circe and her gang. Same old sirens in new costumes, pouring out their poison in teen scene sexploit flicks and viddy sit-corns, or state-of-the-art heavy metal counter-culture rock and roll. Rock and roll my ruddy bum! Lure you onto the rocks and roll you, yer illiterate boobies. Not need no education? Godamighty you're every passin day more and more of yer diein' for need of it.

"And more and more of yer by yer own bleeding hand it seems—is sorta what I wish I would've said. Didn't, of course. Spot of bother in the brain pan. Yer know the difference, incidentally, between a buffalo and a bison? Caint warsh yer fice in a buffalo."

About the shiner . . . Shirly and Faye and I driving in the Nearback, looking for the Outback, took too much of my Inner Skull Balm and found ourselves getting dangerously close to the Faroutback . . . so we concluded we had reached the Let's go back . . . and we headed back through the wine country, saw a ratty looking old sign at the roadby:

FLYSHPECKEN CELLERS
"Con Vivium sluggit downus!"
—pulled into a scrabbly parking lot, shingle over the door of a mock-up of a baronal castle—
"Emil von Flyshpecken & Missus, cheep vinters for God nose how long." I go in, am confronted by the wife, an old sun-gnawed Sheela with one leg missing and a pet dingo on a chain—

"It were him done it, too," she lets me know straight away, giving the chain a viscous jerk. "But I bares 'im no grudge. I were pissed out on the floor and 'e were crashin hungry."

As though prompted to perform an act of contrition, the dingo cringes and commences depositing a great steaming gut-green pile, deadcenter in the doorway. Mrs. Flyschpekkin doesn't notice, her eye cocked contemptiously on me:

"I reckon yerl be wantin a taste of the free Rhine yer seen advertised in the paper. Pah! The only way the old man thinks we can get folks to sample his swill is to offer it on the dole. Well, c'mon. Ach! Goethe! Bad Dingo!"

Gives the chain another jerk and for some reason the beast mistakes me for his tormentor . . . makes a screeching circle around her and charges for my family jewels . . . I starts back in fright and slips in his pile, right on me keester, stuff all over me. She blindsides her pet with the heel of her prosthesis and helps me up, muttering. Her reluctant apologies are cut short by a loud hiss of airbrakes. A big air-conditioned tour bus has pulled into the lot outside. She rushes off to get a shovel, dragging the dingo after her.

I've almost finished scraping the bigger chunks from my pantsleg when the driver of the tourbus—a big Ausie with a red moustache and red hairs bristling from his tanned arms—comes striding through the door. Steps on what's left and slips, butt first, in the pile. He's on his feet immediately, cursing the mess on his driver uniform with such ferocity and frustrated rage that I feel compelled to say something to ease the tension.

"Don't feel bad," I say to him, "I just did that."

And that is how I happened to bring a black eye back from Down Under.

Honestly,

July 14, 2002

Dear Ken,

Thanks for the great letter. I was vastly amused by your stories from Australia. Some of your adventures sound straight out of Laurel and Hardy or the great Chaplin himself. I'd like to see Charlie's version of the great slip-sliding in the doggy poo.

And I appreciated your speaking up for the classics for the young people. I find myself in my own classical mood now, in my mid-sixties. I don't read much contemporary fiction any more. Lots of good stuff being written but these days I prefer to reread the best books that I have already read, written way back there. A lot of great writing has come from Kentucky and the Appalachian region, the coalfields. Same with country music.

You mentioned the Lost Generation. Of course, all literary generations are lost eventually, a few leaving behind enduring stories and pictures. Mr. Cowley's generation was special because it had a scribe in the person of Mr. Cowley himself, who wrote from the inside. How fine it was in 1960–61 to work with Cowley, drink spirits with him, listen to his stories of his World War One generation of American writers. His talk about the "Lost Generation" usually came in answer to somebody's question; he didn't gush about it. Having read Exile's Return on my trip from Kentucky to California to join the writing class, it was thrilling to me when Cowley spoke of "Dos" and "Scott" and "Hem." I didn't even know who "Dos" was until somebody explained it to me. About 1970 I found out that Dos Passos and

Dreiser and Mr. Cowley himself were among a group of radical writers who came to my very own Eastern Kentucky coalfields to investigate the conditions of hungry miners and their families, people chewed up and spat out and terrorized by the great and brutal industrial machine. It's a measure of how dumb I was that I associated with Mr. Cowley that whole year without realizing that he knew far more about my Kentucky region than I did.

Speaking of our Stanford class, it was Frank O'Connor who opened up the Russian writers for me. I seem to remember that you and Mr. O'Connor didn't much like each other. I thought he was great. For me, his remarks on Tolstoy, Turgenev, Chekhov, and Dostoevski opened a whole new world. (I read War and Peace and Anna Karenina back to back over several weeks the summer of 1966 when I was a lookout for the US Forest Service on Sisi Butte, elev. about 7000 feet, there between Mount Hood and Mount Jefferson. Every evening as the sun went down behind Bull 'O The Woods and the whole Cascade range to the west, I sat out on the catwalk sixty feet above the ground and read fifty pages a day. Talk about ideal reading conditions!) In our Stanford class we were serious literary students and practitioners, some of us pretty advanced, some like me raw and green, but all of us ambitious to live our lives by The Word, one way or another.

Best conversation on the planet. After class we'd all go over to the Cellar coffee shop on the campus and hang with Cowley and O'Connor, and most importantly, with ourselves, each other, and talk for hours. Then some of us would come on over to Perry Lane for rice and beans with Faye and new family member Shannon and more good talk until the wine took hold and out would come a guitar and we'd sing awhile, Rock Island line is the road to ride . . . get your tickets at the station . . . wooo woooooo!

People don't use the term "Word" much anymore, a sign of the times. In later years, no matter how our cultural participations and public prankings and visionary experiences played out over time, we always knew that The Word was the core of it all. More than anything else, Ken, and in spite of all, The Word has always been the main thing you and I had in common. In the weirdest of scenes, our common subject still was writing and reading, and good talks.

I remember driving you home after some wild party somewhere, and we were talking about A. B. Guthrie, The Way West, The Big Sky. It was one a.m. or after. The night was cool and clear. The problem was that someone had smashed the windshield with a blunt instrument and it was not entirely easy to see through the spider-webbed glass. I eased through a stop sign, and a cop out of nowhere pulled us over and in the dreaded monotone of cops he said may I see your driver's license please? The ritual began. Have you been drinking? said the cop. I said we've been to a party, officer. I'm just driving my friend home. Do you men live on the campus? he said, and I said, yessir, we're just about home, which lie was at least crime number four for the evening and maybe five or six. You leaned across and said, he's not drunk, officer. He's just driving me back to the frat house. Are you sure? said the cop and we both said we were quite sure. He said then what's that bottle of wine doing on your front seat there? We'd both forgotten it, but there it was, a gallon jug of burgundy, half full. Would you step out of the car please? the policeman said to me, and I got out and went through the various tests and drills and sobriety exercises, walking the line, taking three deep breaths and tilting my head back and looking up at the stars and bringing my hand around in a wide arc to touch the tip of my forefinger to my nose. Somehow I passed his tests. It was a miracle. Can you see to drive? Oh yes, officer. I'm just driving my friend here to his frat house. You're sure all is well for you to drive? I said, yessir, and he said so what's wrong with your glasses? I said nothing, and he said take them off and look at them. Lo! Both lens were smashed beyond repair, broken at the party, stepped on by drunken dancers most likely, spider-webbed, a thousand wrinkled lines going out in all directions from a central point that was pure glass powder by now.

The windshield was fine.

173

When I looked at the policeman again he had a big grin on his face. Go home, he said. Get some sleep. We were only ten feet from the campus. Smashed though they were, I put my glasses back on, started the engine, thanked the officer, and slowly, carefully drove onto the campus that had changed our lives, crossed it to El Camino, then headed for God's own ultimate fraternity row, Perry Lane.

When we were in New York together that time, July 1985, working it out with Viking regarding Demon Box, we talked about how easy it is to stray from the Creative Path and get lost in the secular world of secondary effects. "Losing your lip" you called it, a horn-blower's term, and you talked about the struggle to get it back after not using it often enough, or well enough, or carefully enough. In a sense, Demon Box had to do with getting one's lip back and using it for something original. I think about that now whenever my own lip is lost, hiding somewhere. Perhaps these are the reasons why I have always felt close to Demon Box, almost an orphan book in the eyes of the world. Working with you and Chuck Verrill, the Viking editor, those months in the very bowels of the thing, I knew that it was a significant book. I knew that it was destined to be misunderstood, especially by people who bring their own mental grids and strict models and absolute attitudes to the reading instead of leaving all models at the door and entering the book to see what unknown thing is there. It's not a sixties book. Some people just couldn't lay the sixties model down. It is a seventies-eighties book, of that era, post-sixties. I appreciate Demon Box because it fits no category, because it is loaded with surprises, because of the way it gives us flashes of your own head that are less familiar to readers, and I appreciate it for the wit and the fine writing in it, the words and phrases, the characters. The language is humorous, free in spirit, carnivalesque. It is non-fiction, but it's more complex than that; there is something elusive between fiction and non-fiction, another space for another kind of story

Your letter about Australia strikes me in much the same way, and I thank you for it. It could well be a part of Demon Box.

Now I'm laughing, thinking about our New York adventure. If you remember, in spring of 1985, I was nominated by you and accepted by Viking Press to serve as a kind of mediator/ diplomat to help you and Viking to settle your differences, mend your fences, and otherwise work to clear a path for Author and Publisher to bring out a new Kesey book, to be called Demon Box. I remember the exchanges of letters amongst us all in spring 1985, in which both parties invited me to chart a course that would get the job done. Something like that. I agreed, on the grounds that Press and Author do what I said to do for some short length of time. I was even offered a modest honorarium to perform my task.

So as soon as school was out and I had turned in my last grade, I put the Demon Box project on my personal front burner and went to work. As all sides knew, I am a genius in such things. Making trains run on time is something I have been really good at since my Army days 1961–63 at Fort Ord at Monterey when I, along with my colleague Lieutenant Bevirt of Hassler fame, trained troops for the Vietnam buildup while our mutual military colleague, Marine Lieutenant K. Babbs who, while Hassler and I led the trainees in close order drill and right face, left face, and the hand salute a few miles from Big Sur, had already completed an actual tour of duty in DaNang and environs, and come home from the real war zone and changed into civilian clothes and dared to appear with a van-load of various Pranksterish clowns and ruffians including you, Ken, at the 1962 Salinas Rodeo where I and one sergeant had escorted 200 of my very own troops from Company B, Second Battalion, First Brigade, in their fourth week of training and after which, as was completely normal and by the book, had our troops formed up and otherwise organized to load Army buses for the return ride to Ord fifteen miles away, when you, Ken, and Babbs and several other future Pranksters in full don't-trust-us mode walked out in front of the assembled company, five bus-loads of American soldiers in 1962, and proceeded to give commands to MY PERSONAL SOLDIERS! Babbs was an honest veteran but the rest of you guys hadn't even been in ROTC!

Troops laughing, saluting with the wrong hand, about-facing into each other, stumbling, staggering around, half a squad here marching left-oblique toward the gate of the big arena beyond which lay the fleshpots of Salinas, another squad doing do-si-dos while counting cadence into the wind while still others sang the famous song that all recruits sing after four weeks of training, "We're Lieutenant Norman's soldiers, we're raiders of the night, we're dirty sonsabitches, we'd rather f__ than fight . . ."

This was more than bad behavior, Ken, this was mutiny! Crazed civilians taking command of a unit of the US Army, this was disruption of the ordered world. And it was happening on my watch! In public! What did I do? With a quick exchange of salutes I turned the company over to the sergeant and climbed on the bus with you nut cases. It was the only way to reclaim my dignity.

So in 1985 you and I flew to New York to meet the new Viking editors. Viking treated us nicely, meetings and lunches, early work on the DB material with the sterling Chuck Verrill. We encamped three or four days at the Gramercy Park Hotel, walked the streets for hours together, deep in literary talk. We assigned each other mythic names for our outings. You named me Franchot Tone. I named you King Kong. It was a bit uncanny that we chose perfect names and personas for each other. Even though we both claimed to be middle-age gentlemen of some distinction, there was no getting around the fact that neither of us were natural New Yorkers. Kentucky coal mines, Oregon logwoods. We needed to be in a story of our own making, to be mythologizing, narrating, dramatizing, playing. Play was what it was all about, in a sense. Assuming roles as a means of meeting reality, not head-on, but craftily, playfully. As Franchot Tone I got to let my natural savoir-faire shine. Graceful, elegant, sophisticated, white-jacketed, night-clubbing New Yorker that I was, I said one evening, "King, if you weren't a big ol' ape we'd have dinner at the Stork Club," to which you replied, "And if you weren't a skinny effete white man, we'd tear the Stork Club down."

As soon as we had spoken, we rounded a corner and found a perfect view of the Empire State Building, not ten blocks away. Naturally. How could we not see that building at that precise moment? What is the mythic dimension all about? It was like the time you and Krassner and I were walking along the beach in San Francisco one afternoon in the mid-seventies, all three of us muttering about our frustrations with writing. Where were the words? We managed to not use the dreaded word "blocked." I was carrying my new pocket binoculars, looking out into the ocean, at other people along the beach, the seagulls, the buildings in the background. You borrowed the glasses and looked around, then handed them to Krassner. Paul moved the glasses, turning slowly in the sand. Suddenly he stopped, refocused, and stared through the lens. Then he handed the glasses to me and told me to look across an expanse of water in the direction of a spit of land where there was an old wooden fence, nearly covered over by sand. There on a fence post stood a forlorn-looking seagull whose feet were hopelessly entangled in a thicket of string. The bird was wholly immobilized. Clearly it would never fly again. Attached to the string and clutched in the talons of the gull was a thick, oversized pencil, surely fifteen inches long. We each looked at the gull several times more. Then we writers walked on down the beach without a whole lot to say.

Of course I was carrying my new binoculars; I'd only had them a few days. Of course that doomed writer-bird was there when we looked its way through the binoculars. Of course the Empire State Building stood precisely there for King Kong and Franchot Tone to see at that moment.

A few minutes later we went into a restaurant and sat down. The television was playing, some old black-and-white movie. It really happened. Surely you remember, Ken: There above us on the TV screen was King Kong himself, hanging off the side of the Empire State Building, tiny Fay Wray in his big hairy hand, the fighter planes pumping bullets without end into the giant ape's body. You and I looked at each other and grinned a little. Of

course that movie was playing, that particular scene showing. That's what living in the mythic consciousness is all about.

We drove out of New York and made our way to Philadelphia to see the huge exhibit of Chagall's major work. Hanging on the walls. There it was. (You took some good pictures of us and sent me copies, complete with dialogue balloons.) We both paid attention to Chagall's early work, focusing on details of local village life, country boys that we were.

Then we went to Independence Hall and, to our surprise, it turned out that it was the Fourth of July! Parades, bands, bunting, flags, throngs of people on the streets. I remembered that I love America, air-conditioned nightmare that it is, speaking of Miller. After I dropped you off at the Philadelphia airport for your flight across the continent to Eugene, I drove on south through the Virginia valley, then into the Appalachians, across the Holston River, the Clinch, the Powell, through Pound Gap into my old homeplace, the Eastern Kentucky coalfields.

America indeed.

Your pal, Gurney

In August of 1999, Channel 4, the U.K. commercial television network, sponsored a month-long trip through the British Isles for Kesey, the latter-day Further, and the Merry Pranksters, for the purpose of making a documentary of Further and its high-spirited denizens traveling, performing, and interacting with local populations for Channel 4's Summer of Love Anniversary programmes. "The Last Great Bus Trip," as Kesey all-too-presciently called it, would take Ken and the Pranksters and a large entourage of videographers, filmmakers, producers, and their various support crews on a grand month-long adventure through England, Wales, Ireland, and Scotland.

But before any of that could happen, the Bus had to undertake a seven-week sea voyage, all by its lonesome. Candace Lambrecht, a long-time Prankster who was actively involved in planning and organizing the England trip, also helped to make the arrangements for Further's journey. She lives in San Jose.

FURTHER GOES TO SEA

By Candace Lambrecht

Negotiating my car through the endless snarl of evening traffic around San Francisco International Airport, I had barely paused long enough to scoop up Ken Kesey and his enormous TV camera with its protruding two-foot lens. A few minutes later, as we headed over the Bay Bridge for Oakland, I pointed to the arc lights on the docks, a short landfall away from Treasure Island.

"We're going there."

Our destination was the dock where Further, chained in a secure but eerily Promethean manner to a lowboy, was scheduled to be stowed amidships that very night for debarkation to England. We *had* to shoot this.

There was a full moon, and the dock's water-level view around the Bay to the lit, floating City, tethered with diamond bridges, glowed with expansive magic. The sheer height of the docked ships and Trojan Horse overhead cranes, the roar of trucks, forklifts, diesels of all sorts, tugs, whistles, horns, buzzers, alarms, the brittle blue glare over everything . . . we were overwhelmed, our hearts were in our throats.

Ken and I met our cohort Freddy, who would be helping us film this event, and the cooperative port management team, and donned safety vests and hard hats; we were ready to be ferried into the maelstrom. I had done a few weeks of advance work to get us this far, actually close to the Bus, the much-cleaned, inspected, Customs-cleared, re-packed and battened-down Bus.

The loading plan was a thoroughly engineered event that called for the overhead crane to switch attachment modes to four long chains hooked to each corner of the lowboy. As the crane made the modal switch, a five-ton magnet attachment crashed right next to Kesey's foot as if it had fallen from the sky. His jaw dropped and his eyes glittered at the raw power and magnitude of this whole scene, electric with danger. It's a good thing we had bodyguards from the port crew, given the speed and choreography of the dock operations—especially since Ken was shouldering that huge broadcast-quality TV camera, shooting every minute of the positioning and staging of the lowboy, seeing only through a lens so he could keep it all in focus.

The Bus never looked better.

Among acres of stacked containers, Further sat isolated near the bow of the ship, twinkling curiously, its curving shapes, layers of art and color at the opposite end of the spectrum from the industrial machine in which it was poised. It looked soft, antique, and dear. "Much too vulnerable to the crushes of this brawny place," read Kesey's look.

The port managers had been intrigued by our request to get footage. Ken's legend and that of the Bus delighted the many people involved in the weeks of preparation required to ship such an object. The project had gained new fame at each stage of the process. By loading time, we had quite a group of port management folks escorting us, all nearly as excited as we were at the risk of hoisting this swinging platform hundreds of feet in the air. Lots of stories of dropped yachts and the like. We had to plant our feet against the wind and the buffeting of giant vehicles.

I have never seen Kesey so enthralled, so thrilled.

Never, in all the years of adventures, scraping by every sort of trouble, every sort of Too Much Fun, had Ken's most beloved work of art been so perilously wrested out of his control . . . and boy, was he diggin' it all! "Whattashot!" he was hollering.

The blaring din and flashing starbright lights made communication just about impossible among our three-person film crew. The crane operator, six stories overhead, whizzed into position, thirty-foot bottom chains whipping about. Latched to the four corners of the Bus platform, the chains suddenly snapped into place as the crane hoisted the whole thing about four feet in the air. The Bus platform now swung like a pendulum, describing an arc of several yards.

There was no way of knowing what Ken was seeing through the lens, or what he was hearing in all the ruckus and racket. The swinging Bus, in its erratic trajectory, came within inches of his head. I kept yelling at him to back up. He did not, of course, give an inch. As the bus careened toward us like a goofy child on a swing, I shoved Ken, huge camera and all, out of its path.

Yowza! Everything on the dock was suddenly very quiet. Everyone stopped working except the crane driver. Kesey began berating me for messing up his shot, but Freddy and I agreed that it was a good thing I had.

Whoosh, and the platform gained altitude, still swinging. The Bus kept rocking as the crane topped off and began lowering it into the hold. Our collective gasp, still and breathless, held until Further was nestled comfortably amidships, dead center, center hold, center stage.

Photo by Freddy Hahne

The noise was a hundred times what we'd heard before. Every one of the aforementioned noisemakers went on full-blast, and all the lights flashed strobe-like over the cheering dock-workers. Far out! Kesey grinned, dealing out handshakes all around.

There was even the part afterward when we scaled the greasy, monumental ship and stood teetering on a twelve-inch ledge above the Bus, to watch the crane tamp in two more containers around it for a snug berth. Finally, with safe transfer into the hands of the rascally Greek captain we met up there in the clanking metal world of seafaring, we left, exhilarated, into the warm midnight.

Kentucky writer Ed McClanahan's friendship with Kesey dates back to 1961. "The Day the Lampshades Breathed" (reprinted here by permission of Gnomon Press) is from his 1985 collection Famous People I Have Known.

THE DAY THE LAMPSHADES BREATHED

By Ed McClanahan

> We must all be foolish
> at times. It is one of
> the conditions of liberty.
> —*Walt Whitman*

Like everybody else who lived in California during the 1960s, I Went Through a Phase. I grew me a mustache and a big wig, and got me some granny glasses and pointy-toed elf boots and bell-bottom britches (which did not, Charles Reich to the contrary notwithstanding, turn my walk into "a kind of dance"; *nothing* could turn my walk into a kind of dance). I threw the Ching, I rocked and I rolled. I ingested illicit substances. I revoluted.

But this was not my first attack of *mal de Californie.* I'd been through it all before.

By way of explanation, let me go all the way back to 1952, just long enough to say that after an uninspired freshman year at Washington & Lee, I moved on for three more uninspired years at Miami of Ohio, where I majored in 3.2 beer and blanket parties on the golf course and published uninspired short stories in the campus lit mag. In 1955, I went to Stanford to try my hand at creative writing in graduate school.

Stanford was too many for me. I lasted just two quarters before I received a note from the chairman of the English Department inviting me to drop by and discuss my highly improbable future as a graduate student. I declined the invitation but took the hint, dropped out, and slunk back home to Kentucky to conclude a brief and embarrassingly undistinguished graduate career at the state university in Lexington. Thence to Oregon, and four years of honest toil at Oregon State College in the freshman composition line.

But California had left its mark on me. For I had gone West the blandest perambulatory tapioca pudding ever poured into a charcoal-gray suit, and I came home six months later in Levi's and cycle boots and twenty-four-hour-a-day shades and an armpit of a goatee and a hairdo that wasn't so much a duck's-ass as it was, say, a sort of cocker spaniel's-ass. I had been to San Francisco and seen the Beatniks in North Beach, I had smoked a genuine reefer, I had sat on the floor drinking cheap Chianti and listening to "City of Glass" on the hi-fi. I'd been Californified to a fare-thee-well, and I'd loved every minute of it.

So when I weaseled my way back into Stanford—and California—in the fall of 1962, via a Wallace Stegner Fellowship in Creative Writing, it was a case of the victim returning to the scene of the outrage, eager for more. Immediately, I sought out my old Stanford roommates, Jim Wolpman and Vic Lovell, who were now, respectively, a newly minted labor lawyer and a grad student in psychology, living next door to each other in a dusty, idyllic little bohemian compound called Perry Lane, just off the Stanford campus. Among their neighbors was Ken Kesey, himself but lately down from Oregon, whose novel *One Flew Over the Cuckoo's Nest* had been published just a year ago and was in fact dedicated to Vic—"who told me dragons did not exist, then led me to their lairs"—for having arranged Ken's enrollment as a test subject in a drug-experiment program at the local VA hospital. And the neighborhood was fairly crawling with writers and artists and students and musicians and mad scientists. It was just what I was looking for: a bad crowd to fall in with. I moved in a couple of blocks down the street, and started my mustache.

In a lot of ways, it was the same old California. We still sat on the floor and drank cheap Chianti, though now we listened to Sandy Bull and called the hi-fi a stereo, and the atmosphere was often murky with the sickly-sweet blue smaze of the dread devil's-weed. The manner we'd cultivated back in the fifties was sullen, brooding, withdrawn but volatile, dangerous—if not to others, then at the very least to ourselves. Its models were Elvis, James Dean, Marlon Brando in *The Wild One*. The idea was to seem at once murderous, suicidal . . . and sensitive.

(Locally, our hero in those days had been, improbably enough, the president of the Stanford student-body government, George Ralph, who'd campaigned in sideburns and *Wild One* leathers, behind the sneering slogan "I Hate Cops." George's campaign was a put-on, of course—between those sideburns was a dyed-in-the-wool Stevenson Democrat—but he had the style down cold, and he beat the cashmere socks off the poor Fraternity Row creampuff who opposed him.)

But six years can wreak a lot of changes, and by 1962 the future was already happening again on Perry Lane. "We pioneered"—Vic was to write years later, with becoming modesty— "what have since become the hallmarks of hippie culture: LSD and other psychedelics too numerous to mention, body painting, light shows and mixed-media presentations, total aestheticism, be-ins, exotic costumes, strobe lights, sexual mayhem, freakouts and the deification of psychoticism, Eastern mysticism, and the rebirth of hair." Oh, they *wanted* to maintain their cool, these pioneers, they wanted to go on being—or seeming—aloof and cynical and hip and antisocial, but they just couldn't keep a straight face. They were like new lovers, or newly expectant mothers; they had this big, wonderful secret, and their idiot grins kept giving it away. They were the sweetest, smartest, liveliest, craziest bad crowd I'd ever had the good fortune to fall in with. And their great secret was simply this: They knew how to change the world.

"Think of it this way," my Perry Lane friend Peter, who never drew an unstoned breath, once countered when I mentioned that my TV was on the fritz. "Your TV's all right, but you've been *lookin'* at it wrong, man, you've been bum-trippin' your own TV set!"

For a while there, it almost seemed as if it might really be that easy. The way to change the world was just to start looking at it right, to stop bumming it out (ah, we could turn a phrase in those days!) and start grooving on it—to scarf down a little something from the psychedelicatessen and settle back and watch the world do its ineluctable thing. Gratified by the attention, the world would spring to life and cheerfully reveal its deepest mysteries. The commonplace would become marvelous; you could take the pulse of a rock, listen to the heartbeat of a tree, feel the hot breath of a butterfly against your cheek. ("So I took this pill," said another friend, reporting back after his first visit to the Lane, "and a little later I was lying on the couch, when I noticed that the lampshade had begun to breath . . .") It was a time of what now seems astonishing innocence, before Watergate or Woodstock or Vietnam or Charles Manson or the Summer of Love or Groovy and Linda or the Long, Hot Summer or even, for a while, Lee Harvey Oswald, a time when wonder was the order of the day. One noticed one's friends (not to mention oneself) saying "Oh wow!" with almost reflexive frequency; and the cry that was to become the "Excelsior!" of the Day-Glo Decade, the ecstatic, ubiquitous "Far out!" rang oft upon the air.

The first time I ever felt entitled to employ that rallying cry was on Thanksgiving of 1962. That evening, after a huge communal Thanksgiving feast at the Keseys', Ken led me to his medicine cabinet, made a selection, and said matter-of-factly, "Here, take this, we're going to the movies." A scant few minutes later he and I and three or four other lunatics were sitting way down front in a crowded Palo Alto theater, and the opening credits of *West Side Story* were disintegrating before my eyes. "This is . . . CINERAMA!!" roared the voice-over inside my head as I cringed in my seat. And though I stared almost unblinking at the screen for the next two hours and thirty-five minutes, I never saw a coherent moment of the movie. What I saw was a ceaseless barrage of guns, knives, policemen, and lurid gouts of eyeball-searing color, accompanied by an earsplitting, cacophonous din, throughout which I sat transfixed with terror— perfectly immobile, the other told me afterward; stark, staring immobile, petrified, trepanned, stricken by the certainty, the absolute *certainty,* that in one more instant the Authorities would be arriving to seize me and drag me up the aisle and off to the nearest madhouse. It was the distillation of all the fear I'd ever known, fear without tangible reason or cause or occasion, pure, unadulterated, abject Fear Itself, and for one hundred and fifty-five awful minutes it invaded me to the very follicles of my mustache.

Then, suddenly and miraculously, like a beacon in the Dark Night of the Soul, the words "The End" shimmered before me on the screen. Relief swept over me, sweet as a zephyr. I was delivered. The curtain closed, the lights came up. I felt grand, exuberant, triumphant—as if I'd just ridden a Brahma bull instead of a little old tab of psilocybin. If they'd turned off the lights again I'd have glowed in the dark. Beside me, Ken stood up and stretched.

"So how was it?" he inquired, grinning.

"Oh wow!" I croaked joyfully. "It was fa-a-r out!"

And in that instant, for me, the sixties began. Characteristically, I was about two years later getting out of the gate, but I was off at last.

Ken Kesey was, and is, a singular person, as all who know him will attest. But these were *all* singular people, this lunatic fringe on Stanford's stiff upper lip. I should probably keep this to myself, but to tell the truth, the thing I remember best about the next few years is the parties. We had the swellest parties! Parties as good as your childhood birthday parties were supposed to be but never were, outrageously good parties, parties so good that people would sometimes actually forget to drink!

The best parties were immaculately spontaneous. Typically, they began with some Perry Lane denizen sitting at the breakfast table, staring out the kitchen window into the dappled, mellow perfection of a sunny California Saturday morning, resolving: Today, I'm gonna take a little trip. By early afternoon, two or three friends would have dropped by and signed on for the voyage, and together they'd choke down either some encapsulated chemical with an appetizing title like URP-127, or an equally savory "natural" concoction like peyote-orange juice up-chuck or morning-glory seeds with cream and sugar (don't try it, reader; it ain't Grape-Nuts, and there's nothing natural about it), and then for the next half hour or so they'd lie around trying not to throw up while they waited for the lampshades to start respirating. A similar scene was liable to be transpiring in two or three other Perry Lane households at the same time, and it wouldn't be long till every lampshade in the neighborhood was panting like a puffer-belly. The incipient party would have begun to assert itself.

Under the giant oak by Vic's front door—the very oak in whose shade Thorstein Veblen was alleged to have written *The Theory of the Leisure Class*—half a dozen solid citizens with pinwheel eyeballs might be banging out an aboriginal but curiously copacetic sort of hincty bebop on upturned wastebaskets, pots and pans, maybe an old set of bongos left over from the fifties, Vic himself laying down the basic bop lines on his favorite axe, a pocket-comb-and-tissue-paper humazoo. Next door at the Keseys', they'd have drawn the blinds and hung blankets over the windows, and Roy Sebern, a wonderfully hairy artist who lived, apparently on air, in a tiny box on the back of his pickup in a succession of backyards, would be demonstrating his newest creation, a rickety contraption that projected amorphous throbbing blobs of luminous color all over the walls and ceiling, like lambent, living wallpaper, to the murmuring chorus of oh-wows and far-outs that issued from an audience of several puddles of psychedelicized sensibility on the Kesey carpet. Over at my house on Alpine Road, Peter and I were feverishly juicing peyote buttons in my wife's brand-new Osterizer.

In the late afternoon, Gurney Norman, another apprentice writer from Kentucky, might turn up, sprung from Fort Ord on a weekend pass. Gurney had made his way to Stanford and Perry Lane a couple of years earlier (it was he, in fact, who'd spotted the original breathing lampshade), and had then gone into the army to complete an ROTC obligation, and promptly bounced back to California in the guise of a first lieutenant, running recruits through basic training down at Ord during the week and expanding his horizons at Perry Lane on the weekends. The military was doing great things for Gurney's organizational skills; within minutes of his arrival he'd have a squad of giggling beardy-weirdies and stoned Perry Lane–style WACS in muumuus hut-hoop-hreep-hoing up and down the street with mops and broomsticks on their shoulders, in an irreverent gloss on the whole idea of close-order drill.

Eventually the party would assemble itself somewhere, more than likely around the corner at Chloe Scott's house, to take on victuals and cheap Chianti. Chloe is at all odds the most glamorous woman I've ever known. A professional dancer and dance teacher, redheaded and fiery, a real knockout and a woman of the world, Chloe Kiely-Peach of the British gentry by birth, daughter of a captain in the Royal Navy, she'd come to America, to New York, as a girl, during the Blitz, and had stayed on to become, in the early fifties, part of Jackson Pollock's notoriously high-spirited East Hampton social circle. Along the way she married a dashing young naturalist and spent a year on the Audubon Society's houseboat in the Everglades, fell briefly under the spell of a Reichian therapist and basted herself in an orgone box, and at last, divorced, made her way west to settle in as one of the reigning free spirits on Perry Lane. At Chloe's, anything could happen.

And, as they say, usually did. For starters, Neal Cassady might fall by, the Real Neal, Kerouac's pal and the prototype for Dean Moriarty of *On the Road*, trailing adoring fallen women and authentic North Beach beatniks in his wake, looking like Paul Newman and talking as if he'd been shooting speed with a phonograph needle—which, come to think of it, he probably had: "Just passing through, folks, don't mind us, my shed-yool just happened to coincide with Mr. Kesey's here, and all that redundancy, you understand, not to mention the works of Alfred Lord Tennyson and the worst of the poems of Schiller, huntin' and peckin' away there as they did, except of course insofar as where you draw the line, that is, but in any case I believe it was at, let me see, Sebring, yes, when Fangio, with the exhaust valves wide open and the petcocks too that you've sometimes seen, starting with Wordsworth, you see, and working backward, in the traditional fashion, straight through Pliny the elder and *beyond*, though it's much the same with the fusion of the existential and the transcendental, or, if you will, the universal and the transmission, as in the case of the 1940 flat-head Cadillac 8, why, you naturally get your *velocity* mixed up with your *veracity*, of course, and who *knows* what that's cost us? So I'll just say how-d'ye-do to my friend Mr. Kesey here, and then we'll be on our way, have to get there in plenty of time, you understand . . ." Neal never stuck around for long, but he was terrific while he lasted.

Then there was Lee Anderson, a roly-poly, merry little apple dumpling of a Ph.D. candidate in some obscure scientific discipline at Stanford, who could sometimes, at very good parties, be prevailed upon to . . . play himself! Bowing to popular demand, blushing bashfully from head to toe, Lee would strip down to his skivvies (an effective attention-getting device at any party), wait for silence, and at last begin rhythmically bobbing up and down to some inner tempo, as though he were about to improvise a solo on an invisible stand-up bass, now lightly slapping himself with his open hands on his plump little thighs and roseate tummy—*slappity-slappity-slappity-slap*—now cupping one hand in his armpit and flapping the arm to produce a small farting sound, like a tiny tuba—*slappity-slappity-poot-poot slappity-poot, slappity-poot*—now shaping his mouth into an oval and rapping on his skull with the knuckles of first one hand, then the other, then both, making of his mouth a sort of reverb chamber—*pocketa-pock, pocketa-pock, pocketa-pecketa-pucketa-pock*—picking up the tempo, working furiously, sweat flying, the whole ensemble tuning in—*slappity-pock, slappity-pock, slappity-pocketa-poot, slappity-pocketa-poot, pocketa-poot, pocketa-pecketa-poot, pecketa-pucketa-poot, slappity-pucketa-poot-poot, slappity-pucketa-poot-poot* . . . It wasn't the New York Philharmonic, maybe, but Lee's was a class act just the same—as Dr. Johnson might have put it, the wonder was not that he did it well, but simply that he could do it at all—and it always brought the house down.

I'm not exactly sure what Vic means by "sexual mayhem," so I won't try either to confirm or to deny it. I'll just say that during one party I opened the door to the darkened bedroom where the coats were piled on the bed and heard a muffled female voice say from the darkness, "Close the door, please, Ed. We're fucking in here."

Basically, though, the parties were just good, clean, demented fun. At any moment the front door might burst open and into the celebrants' midst would fly Anita Wolpman, Jim's wife, with the collar of her turtleneck sweater pulled up over her head, hotly pursued by Jim, brandishing an ax gory with ketchup. Or Bob Stone, a splendid writer who has also done some Shakespeare on the stage, might suddenly be striding about the room delivering himself, with Orson Wellesian bombast and fustian, of an impromptu soliloquy, a volatile, unreproducibly brilliant admixture of equal parts Bard, King James Bible, *Finnegan's Wake,* and (so I always suspected) Bob Stone. Or Lorrie Payne, a madcap Australian jack-of-all-arts, might wander in with a skinned green grape stuffed halfway into one nostril and part the horrified multitudes before him like an exhibitionist at a DAR convention. Or one might find oneself—literally find oneself—engaged in one or another of the goofy conversations that would be ensuing in every corner of the house, as did Gurney and I the night we determined that behind the pegboard on Chloe's kitchen wall lurked an enormous baby chick, ready to pounce on us, bellowing, in a voice like

Bullmoose Jackson's, "PEEP! PEEP!" Or somebody might cut open an old golf ball and start unwinding the endless rubber band inside, and in moments a roomful of merrymakers would be hopelessly ensnarled in a rubbery web, writhing hilariously—a surreal tableau which, to my peyote-enchanted eyes, was astonishingly beautiful, and was entitled *We're All in This Thing Together.*

At one party, Gurney maneuvered ten delirious revelers into the backyard, looped Chloe's fifty-foot clothesline about them, and endeavored to create the World's Largest Cat's Cradle. "Awright now, men," he kept bawling at his troops, "I want all the thumbs to raise their hands!"

Well, okay, you had to be there. No denying there was plenty of unmitigated adolescent silliness in all those high jinks—just as there's no denying the unfortunate similarity between my experience at *West Side Story* and that of the celebrated Little Moron, the one who beats himself on the head with a hammer because it feels so good to stop. But like the man in the aftershave commercial, we *needed* that, some of us, to wake us from the torpor of the fifties. To be sure, there were casualties—those who couldn't put the hammer down till they'd pounded their poor heads to jelly, those who blissed out or blasted off, those for whom dope was a purgative and every trip a bad trip, an exorcism. And I'm also perfectly willing to concede, if I must, that there were just as many others who successfully expanded their consciousnesses to wonderful dimensions through the miracle of chemistry.

But for weekenders and day-trippers like me, psychedelics were mostly just for laughs; they made things more funny ha-ha than funny-peculiar. And for me at least, the laughter was a value in itself. I hadn't laughed so unrestrainedly since childhood, and the effect was refreshing, bracing, invigorating—aftershave for the psyche. Nor had I ever in my life allowed myself to fall so utterly in love with all my friends at once. And there were several occasions, in the highest, clearest moments of those high old times, when I caught a glimpse of something at the periphery of my vision that shook the throne of the tyrannical little atheist who sat in my head and ruled my Kentucky Methodist heart.

It was all too good to last, of course. Quick as the wink of a strobe light, Kennedy had fallen to Lee Harvey Oswald, the Vietnam issue was as hot as a two-dollar pistol, the country was a-boil with racial unrest . . . and Perry Lane had gone under to the developers. The times, they were a-changin', and not for the better, either. The first day of the rest of our lives was over.

Kathryn Lawder of San Diego wrote "Now THAT'S Ken Kesey!" shortly after Ken's death. Mahrie, her daughter, is now a student at Carleton College in Minnesota.

"NOW *THAT'S* KEN KESEY!"

By Kathryn Lawder

My daughter was ten and Ken was collaborating with the Portland Symphony to present *Little Tricker the Squirrel Meets Big Double the Bear.* I brought my daughter into the big city from our rural farm community near Aurora to see the performance and to see Ken Kesey.

When the concert master appears, violin tucked under his arm, to take his seat and the audience applauds, little Miss Mahrie leans over to me and in a stage whisper asks:

"Is that Ken Kesey?"

"No, honey, you wait, he'll be on in a while."

The conductor appears, and again Mahrie asks:

"Is that Ken Kesey?"

"No, sweetie. I tell you what: When Ken Kesey walks out onto the stage, you won't have to ask me, you'll know."

"How will I know?"

"I don't know how, but I'm sure we'll recognize him."

The first half of the concert proceeds, followed by intermission, followed by the reappearance of concert master and conductor.

At long last, onto the stage emerges—larger than life, in full tails, a GIANT bear head with a jaunty top hat perched on high—a . . . presence. He swaggers out onto the stage.

Mahrie, with a HUGE smile on her face, turns to me, nods emphatically, and says:

"Now THAT's Ken Kesey!

A FOOTNOTE: Kathryn Lawder's affectionate recollection is one of dozens of such stories and messages posted on www.pranksterweb.org, a website run by Rick Dodgson (see p.125) which has become something of an electronic archive of Prankster history. When Kesey died, many people whose lives had been touched by him sent memories and messages of tribute directly to pranksterweb, and many others were forwarded there by Ken Babbs from IntrepidTrips.com, the Pranksters own (now defunct) website. All are now permanently displayed on pranksterweb.

Two other websites of special interest: Zane and Stephanie Kesey's www.Key-Z.com offers Kesiana of every description for sale—books (some signed by the author), videos, tapes, and Prankster art and artifacts. Ken Babbs's www.skypilotclub.com (see p.54) is a valuable (and entertaining) source of information about ongoing Prankster activities.

Robert Stone spoke eloquently, without notes, at the 92nd Street Y tribute to Kesey in New York on February 11, 2002 (see p. 120). "The Boys Octet" is adapted from his remarks. Stone's latest novel is Bay of Souls.

THE BOYS OCTET

By Robert Stone

It's always extremely difficult to look back on someone's life and try to choose the aspect of it that seems most to lend itself to celebration. I have here a copy of *Sometimes a Great Notion,* which I have always felt was Kesey's greatest novel. It shows a picture of that intense, thoughtful Kesey who is gazing into space, who seems to be stalking something, who seems to have spotted something. The Kesey who is always associated with quotes like "There is great ear out there, and it is always open."

And I remember him saying that to me once—that there is a great ear out there and it is always open. To tell you the truth, this is not the kind of thing that I enjoy people telling me. I am uneasy with that kind of cosmic ambition, even in ordinary conversation. But I know the level on which Kesey believed that, and the ways in which he chose to pursue it, the ways in which he tried to come to terms with those forces in the world that are beyond us, were in a way unique to him. I do not think anybody ever struggled so hard and so overtly, so *physically,* with the forces beyond us, since Jacob at Peniel.

The dedication of *Sometimes a Great Notion* reads "To my mother and father—Who told me songs were for the birds, / Then taught me all the tunes I know / And a good deal of the words." And his dedication of *One Flew Over the Cuckoo's Nest* is to our mutual friend Vic Lovell, a psychologist in California ". . . who told me dragons did not exist, / then led me to their lairs." There is a kind of contradiction there, the idea of a young man—a boy who was turning into a young man—who was ready to see through all these pretensions that the world made for creation and the act of creation, until he could experience it himself—until he *did* experience it himself. In other words, until he made it his own, until he made the process his own. I think that belief was a very important thing to him, but I don't think he believed in anything that he could not somehow make his own in a sense—not dominate, but simply make his own.

I first met him in 1962. He published two novels in what seemed to be an amazingly short time, two years, and then set out on that original bus trip to the World's Fair in 1964. Those who went had that as their purpose. Probably [that period] was the absolute zenith of American power and wealth. At that same time it was an era of tremendous discontent, which he represented. He felt and represented that discontent. In the very nature of the prosperity, of the tremendous feeling of power, there was a kind of discontent. I don't think he could quite put his finger on it. I think he wanted to go to New York, to the World's Fair, to kind of protest the nature of these blessings that we were all enjoying.

I think he wanted to somehow short-circuit the necessities of art. I think he believed that he could somehow invent a spiritual technology, an applied spiritual technology, somewhere between Silva mind control and the transistor, that would spare all the humiliating labor that went into the creating of art. I think he thought that a lot of basic metaphysical mistakes have been made about the world, and that they could be righted.

And I think that when he came into the world of drugs, he really saw in them a means, a formula. I don't know how many people here have read *Dr. Jekyll and Mister Hyde*. *Dr. Jekyll and Mister Hyde* is a great book, truly one of the great novellas in English. It is both a Calvinist moral story and a science fiction story. It could apply very well to Kesey, because those were elements that made up his life.

But when we set forth with him—and when you went out with him, you always had the sense of Setting Forth; you didn't just go somewhere, you Set Forth—it was as though we were out to resolve whatever had been overlooked between where we were and where we ought to be. I never knew anyone in my life, before or since, who was a dreamer on that scale, who really believed in Possibility, the great American bugbear Possibility, to the degree that Kesey did. I never knew anyone who had his ability to communicate that sense of Possibility. He was not, I think, enough of an individualist by nature to want to become a novelist. I think he had preferred acting when he was starting out, and I think he disliked the loneliness and the isolation of the writer's life, and he was determined to somehow make it all happen faster for everybody.

And at this point, just as the bus trip gets under way, the nature of America begins to change and the assassinations take place, the Kennedy assassination takes place, and all the feelings of security and the certainties that, in a certain way, Kesey was rebelling against are taken from us, and we are visited with a confusion, which I think Ken refused to accept. I think Ken saw, or believed, that America in the late first half of the century had reached a point that it was meant to be at, and that its arts, its thinking, all of these could be carried almost by main force, if enough people believed in it, into another dimension.

He was a true dreamer. But unlike a lot of dreamers who had dreams on his scale and dimension, he was also a person of innate goodness, which is tremendously important for us [to note] while we are remembering him here, because Kesey could be quoted out of context in ways that made him seem more purely interested in power than he was. He had a good heart. He desired good things for people, for all sorts of people.

I remember we were both reading here one night in 1992; we were introducing each other, and he recalled a night in the Albert Hall, Christmas Eve in the Albert Hall in London. He was telling a humorous anecdote about me—which isn't always easy. He said it was Christmas Eve and the Beatles were there and everyone was having fun, and Stone started singing *Deutschland über Alles*. You will understand: I was not happy. I had started singing the *Internationale*, not *Deutschland über Alles*. I am happy to finally clear that one up.

He was a great artist, whose best work is going to last as some of the exemplary work of the twentieth century. . . . I think anybody who met him and had to do with him has got to say, as [the previous speaker] said, "Thanks, thanks for that encounter."

You know Ken had a little joke, a little jingle on himself. He said, "Of offering more than what I can deliver, I have a bad habit, it's true. / But I have to offer more than what I can deliver, to be able to deliver what I do." Maybe that is true of everybody.

There was another nonsense song that we used to sing [in the Perry Lane days]. We decided—there were about eleven or twelve of us, boys and girls—we decided that we were the Boys Octet. So we had a little anthem that we sang, our mixed-gender, eleven-or-twelve-member Boys Octet. We used to sing, "I never had such a good time yet / As when I was a member of the Boys Octet."

David Stanford (see p. 120) is a freelance book editor and a content provider/editor for uclick. He lives in Amenia, NY.

WORKING WITH KESEY

By David Stanford

I Ching:
64. Wei Chi / BEFORE COMPLETION
It points to the fact that every end contains a new beginning.
Thus it gives hope.
Friends foregather in an atmosphere of mutual trust.

Not long after my arrival at Viking Penguin in 1988, Kesey's editor Chuck Verrill left, and I was delighted to find myself overseeing the final stages of the novel *Caverns*. Written by Kesey and his graduate writing seminar, known collectively as "O.U. Levon," the adventure yarn was on the 1990 list. The class was nearing the end of its year-long mission—to write and publish a novel—and as part of the experience I thought they should have a session with an editor. In June 1989, when it was time to nail down the cover concept, I took my first trip to Pleasant Hill and stayed with Ken and Faye at the farm. Over dinner and a long relaxed evening I talked with the class about the rest of the publication process and looked at the artwork they'd created. The poster advertising the public reading from the completed manuscript was a linoleum block print featuring Native American petroglyphs, which figured in the tale. Ken's idea was to use this art for the book cover. We just needed to play around with the type and add all the names of the O.U. Levon crew. He thought it would be best if we could hand-print an actual piece of art that would serve as the cover and just have Penguin photograph it. An artist by avocation, with a bit of linoleum block experience, I was happy to volunteer for the task, and returned to Hoboken with the heavy slabs in my bag.

I spent a long weekend session in the kitchen, carving on the blocks and creating some separate background color-fields. I painstakingly tried to print the words and images on top of the background, but couldn't get everything to come out perfectly. In the end we had to settle for a simulation. I took the best print and doctored it up a bit with pen and ink, and gave it and a background painting to the art director. Putting them together to make the finished image was easy for him. Ken and I shared a cover credit.

I mention this story because it set the tone for being Ken's editor over the next twelve years—that he would think hand-printing a book cover made sense and that I would enjoy trying to help make it happen.

Working with Kesey felt familiar to me, in part because of my own native West Coast sensibilities, but also from the post-college years I'd spent on my cousins' Illinois farm. From this wonderful big hardworking clan I'd learned to love work, and learned that at its best it is about being part of a group of people you like, doing something both mental and physical, with laughter an essential element, improvisation a constant, any material and technique usable for any purpose, everyone devoting their various skills toward the common goal. On the farm everyone carried a pair of pliers, and when corn needed to be scooped, everybody picked up a shovel. As I worked with Kesey on books over the years it was natural to also work on his other creative projects, some of which had book dimensions or potential, and many of which involved his wonderful network of friends and family. Kesey had a fundamental joy-in-work, work-in-joy attitude, which also permeates the whole Prankster crew, independent and multiskilled people who pitch in together on whatever undertaking is at hand.

The problem with writing is that it's solitary work. Kesey had a gift for it, but he also had a lifelong affinity for people and for rituals, theater, magic, music, and fun. "I never wanted to be a writer," he was fond of saying. "I'm a magician. Writing is just one of the tricks I do." Not something a book publisher would be happy to hear, perhaps, but it's essential to take him seriously on this point in order to grasp the scope of his life's work. The books and articles are just part of the overall picture.

By the time *Caverns* came out, we were working on *The Further Inquiry*, a screenplay about the trial of the spirit of Neal Cassady. Was he a force for good or a force for evil? The book was going to be oversized with rich color throughout and Ron "Hassler" Bevirt's photographs from the original 1964 bus trip. The original Furthur had long reposed in an impressive state of ever-increasing noble decrepitude on the farm. It was low on moving parts, but full of living ones—moss and weeds grew in the richly decaying interior. While we were working on the book, Ken had come upon a younger old bus, and a soul transplant was performed, conveying the spirit and a few essential and symbolic parts into a new body. Over at the Creamery it was equipped with a huge roof deck with a windscreen across the front, aluminum-and-web railings, and a ladder in the rear leading down to the wide back porch. Months of careful painting in the bus barn at the farm ensued with long periods of contemplation over what might go where. Image by image, layer by layer, it became more and more impressive, worked on by many creative hands.

The Further Inquiry was due to come out in the fall of 1990, and we planned to announce and promote it in May at the ABA—the huge annual American Booksellers Association convention, to be held that year in Las Vegas. As the new bus became gloriously roadworthy, I urged Ken to bring it to the ABA festivities, and he pitched me a deal. He was set on the idea that the bottom right-hand corner of each page of *The Further Inquiry* would include a frame of black-and-white footage of a shirtless Neal dancing wildly for the camera. If Viking agreed to this "flip book," Further would ride south. Done. In the days before departure I found myself once again at the farm, paint-brushes and acrylics in hand as Ken directed me to the right rear section of the bus, an area still sparsely imaged. I enjoyed several days in art ecstasy before we mounted up for the run down the east side of the Sierra Nevada, via Reno, to Vegas.

The first rainy road day was probably my introduction to the fine art of "coming on." The improvisational verbal pyrotechnics of Neal Cassady have attained legendary status, but Ken Babbs is one of the few people I've seen who's pursued the art form seriously. As we rolled through rural northeastern California he cued up cassettes from the original 1964 bus trip, and rapped spontaneously through and with them, creating new overdubbed tapes. Eventually the bus was equipped with headsets throughout, but on this run the roof was equipped only with a funky field telephone, through which you could communicate with the bridge below, reporting traffic conditions and navigational tips in tricky circumstances. I settled into roof riding, a wind-blown pleasure so intense that I spent most of all the runs I made in subsequent years in the front left corner, tucked in behind the windshield, headphones clamped on, happily glibbeling into the microphone. Especially at night, this wordplay and soundplay is liberating and, in the best of conditions, filled with cosmic surprises. Further is built for fun, and it can bring it out of anyone.

The vast majority of people who encounter the bus don't think of it in terms of Kesey, or the Pranksters, or Neal Cassady. There's no history attached. The bus is just the bus, and I came to understand why Kesey referred to it as his greatest work. Sometimes as a bus trip approached I would find myself slightly unsure. Wasn't it dangerous? Was it crazy to climb up on top and ride it down the freeway? I had a family, small children. It would start to not make complete sense. But as soon as I was settled in on the roof and Kesey would fire up the first song—often "Hit the Road, Jack"—we'd roll onto the road and I would just start smiling. I don't know that I've ever felt safer or more at peace than while riding this big happy beast. On a run you get used to being looked at, because you quickly realize people aren't seeing you. They're seeing the bus. You're almost invisible. You're PART of the bus. People look up and take it in—the color, the shape, the flags, the bubbles, the tootling flutes—and they grin. It's the circus going past, a cloud of music with Newt the Nutcatcher on front, a totem pole on one side, God and Pogo on the other, and "E Pluribus Unum" on the back. It's like riding on a smile.

Photo by Brian Lanker

After our desert passage we twinkled down the blinking pinball streets of Vegas, and in daylight parked next to a patch of lawn outside the ABA. We never made it inside, just sat in the shade and visited with conventioneers, inviting them to Viking's *Further Inquiry* bash, held in a ballroom at one of the big casinos. The event was packed. Kesey, Babbs, and Carolyn Garcia (aka Mountain Girl) spoke about the bus, and about Neal's influence, and Kesey railed against the black Vegas hole, down which America's seniors seemed to be flushing much of the inheritance that in an earlier time would have been handed along to the next generation, perhaps in the form of a small business, or a farm. Then the lights came down, a projector flickered to life, and there on the wall was the great bus barn door hoisting up—the real door in the ballroom wall hoisting up at the same time in the same spot, Further roaring out of the bus barn—and the real Further roaring through the doorway and rolling onto the carpet, bell ringing, noisemakers noisemaking, into the hall amid cheers and music and bubbles. *Vroom! Brrrrrrroom!* with "The Magic Bus" blasting from the speakers. It was a joyful moment, and as I hopped up onto the bus ladder, Peter Mayer, corporate president of Penguin worldwide, caught my eye and pointed at me, grinning, "Now THIS," he said, "is publishing!"

———————

Kesey's next book project, his Alaska novel *Sailor Song*, was long in coming. He'd been a fair way into it when Jed died, which derailed him for some time. On one of my first visits to the farm he handed me a sizable chunk of manuscript.

Several years later, as it neared completion, he was in our neck of the New Jersey waterfront, holed up in an unbearably well-sealed hotel on the Hudson River with a stunning view across to Manhattan. Therese and I lived nearby in Hoboken, and I'd hauled my Selectric II over to the hotel in a cab so we could work through changes as we neared the point where we'd turn it in to production. The evolving *Sailor Song* manuscript was filled with his tight red inkwork, lengthy new passages written out on the backs of pages. We'd been burning up the fax lines for some time, and were now hunkered down retyping the most recently reworked sections.

The airlessness of the hotel proved too much for Ken and we moved operations to our apartment on Bloomfield Street. He slept on the couch, and bonded in the middle of the night with Wild Thing, one of our most unusual cats. It made sense that they would hit it off. Animals are a constant presence in Kesey's life, as in his work. As we talked about book ideas over the years, Kesey would circle round some kind of autobiography. The only way it would ever happen was if he came up with the right unusual angle. At one point he fastened on the idea of telling his life story through the animals in it, beginning almost at the beginning with his first dog. He called me up, enthusiastic about the concept, and by way of illustration read a beautiful journal passage about a boy who'd visited the farm and accidentally killed a bird. One of the smallest animals in his fiction is secretly at the heart of *Sailor Song*. I've never heard anyone mention it. When you read the book, keep an eye out.

During the first years we worked together Kesey published *Caverns*, *The Further Inquiry*, and the children's book *Little Tricker the Squirrel Meets Big Double the Bear*. Teaching writing and working with O.U. Levon had helped ease him back into work, he said, and publishing these titles in fairly tight sequence got him back out in the public eye. He hoped this would make it easier to complete and publish the Alaska book, as the phenomenal success of *Cuckoo* and the high critical regard for *Notion* put tremendous pressure on his next full-blown novel. He worked long and hard on *Sailor Song*, often retreating to the coast house for extended intensive work runs. I offered notes, comments, suggestions, feedback, and encouragement—and steered us through the seemingly inevitable cover struggle.

Although it ended up as the de facto publication party for *Sailor Song*, the "Third Decadenal Field Trip" was by tradition a glorious weekend outdoor Grateful Dead concert near Eugene. Kesey began preparing to offer a "toeliner show" (in counterpoint to the Dead's "headliner" presentation) to entertain campers from a rolling stage on a flatbed truck, and a long line of auditioners made their way to the farm. When, at the tenth or eleventh hour, Jerry Garcia fell ill, Kesey decided to carry on with his portion of the program and set up a stage in the back meadow at the farm. Handkerchiefs were printed for the occasion, reproducing his "Steal Your Feather" event logo, the original of which was painted on a leather hide and stretched on a frame of poles. Poets, bards, bluegrassers, traditional Indian dancers, and rappers performed from morning till night, the show ending with Kesey's full-costume complete-stage-set performance of *The Sea Lion*, the children's story at the heart of *Sailor Song*.

On the parked bus one night, the interior warmly lit by a living room lamp, someone complimented Ken on the book's dedication:

> *To Faye—*
> *A deep keel in the raving waves*
> *A polestar in the dark*
> *A shipmate*

"That's the best thing I ever wrote," he said.

Kesey had a remarkable ability to draw crowds, especially in the West. During the tour in support of *Sailor Song* his appearance at Powell's in Portland, Oregon, drew the biggest audience they'd ever had, as did his talk at Cody's Books in Berkeley. Around this time he reinvented the autographed book, raising the bar considerably. While you're talking to him he's working out of a briefcase that's stuffed with paint and glitter pens, stamp pad and rubber stamps and stickers, gold and silver metallic ink, creating a one-of-a-kind 3-D embossed fluorescent inscription with drop-shadows, a forest, and frogs. After a reading or show Kesey spent hours and hours, not just signing and saying "Thanks," but giving each person his total attention, hearing their story and giving something of himself in return.

Kesey sometimes claimed to be ticking off his "fiction compulsories." *Sailor Song* had been his science fiction novel. The next project—*Last Go Round*—was his Western. Kesey and Babbs collaborated on this clever rodeo buck-'em-up which was based on a true incident at the 1911 Pendleton Roundup. It came out in 1994, accompanied by Kesey's and Babbs's "singing cowboy" tour.

Around this time Kesey returned to his *Jail Journal*, aka "Cut the Motherfuckers Loose." Written and drawn on notebooks in 1967 while he was serving time for a pot bust, he gave it form in the months immediately after his release. His brother Chuck had provided him top-quality 18" x 23" art boards, and Kesey collaged the hand-lettered story onto them, thoroughly intertwining artwork and psychedelic calligraphy. But after dozens of pages were completed it became clear that publishing it was too daunting for Viking or anyone else at the time, and Kesey turned his attention elsewhere. With color printing in larger trim sizes now, in 1997, much cheaper, Viking committed to publishing it and Kesey resumed work on it.

But that and everything else—all intended, begun, and partially completed projects—were shifted to the back burner in decisive deference to the "ritual reality" production *Twister.* This musical play was built on a Wizard of Oz foundation and a sort of nineteenth-century static stage backdrop style to address the seeming unraveling of the world at the end of the twentieth. It was an ambitious undertaking that called on the talents of everyone in Kesey's extended circle, and every inch of it was homemade. Sets were built, effects conceived and created, unique pieces of electronic equipment wired up, costumes sewn, posters and logos drawn. Jambay, a gifted band from Seattle, signed on, along with several professional actor friends who carried some of the lead roles. Emily Messmer, a young Kesey cousin, played the angel who provides the play's cathartic moment of grace.

In *Twister* an augmented Wizard of Oz crew—Kesey as Oz, Carol Provance as Good Witch Glenda, Feivel as Dorothy, George Walker as Tin Man, Phil Dietz as Scarecrow, Ken Babbs as Thor, Simon Babbs as Elvis, Arzinia Richardson as Legba—addressed the impending perils being visited upon the world. Over a two-year period beginning in 1993 the show was performed eighteen times in California, Oregon, Idaho, and Colorado, and most if not all of the performances were filmed. I was able to pitch in with camerawork on the shows at the Fillmore in San Francisco, after which we drove all night to get to an L.A. venue.

There we found ourselves in a too-large auditorium. Technical problems abounded, and despite our eager efforts that day, passing out handbills at the nearby ABA convention, the crowd was thin. But some ABA-ers had made the trek, and those who had shown up seemed keen. As curtain hour drew near, Kesey, typically, was addressing some detail of stagecraft. I think it was Emily's halo—it wasn't hanging right, or wouldn't stay up. With minutes to go, Kesey found a way into the next-door community center and came rushing back to mold a commandeered coat hanger into just the right halo-holding shape.

After the rousing "G-L-O-R-I-A" finale and the signing and the bookselling and the packup, I was outside in the cool air talking with the members of a band who'd come to see the show. As they stuffed themselves into their van and headed off toward a distant gig, I found myself marveling that Kesey, for all his fame, was working on the same drive-all-night, set-up, tear-down, do-it-yourself basis as these young players. Why didn't he turn *Twister* over to professionals, let other people stage it in a more fully realized form, without coathangers to bend, or microphones to repair with duct tape, or nonflashing flashpots? Without all the sweat. But that was exactly the point. Kesey didn't want to go big time. He didn't want to use his success to get Somewhere Else. Where he was was good, and he stayed in his own movie—in his own life. And that life was about touching people directly. In an interview from jail in 1967 he described his job as "bringing light and color into the world," and he kept at it continually. "I got my marching orders," he once told me, "and I'll continue to carry them out until I receive new ones."

It was in this period, and in the spirit of one-on-one contact, that Kesey and Babbs went online, a fact which had helped

211

shape *Twister* and affected a great deal of the work of that decade. From the mid-'90's on, anybody in the world could e-mail Kesey and Babbs and have a good chance of getting a direct reply. Like much of America at that time, they sat at their computers tapping away, dogs under the desk. They posted constantly—pieces by Kesey, long and short, pieces by Babbs, quotes and interesting e-mails, photos, and links. When friend Carol Provance was in desperate need of a bone marrow donor they used www.intrepidtrips.com to help. The site also gave them a way to pre-organize audience participation for *Twister.* Those recruited into joining L.O.S.T.—the Legion of the Sufficiently Twisted—received scripts in advance of *Twister* coming to their town, and arrived at the theater prepared to enact their roles as Twisters, Stompers, or Moaners.

The 1964 bus trip had created a legacy of raw material—miles of audiotape and a massive heap of 16-mm footage that had defied numerous courageous editing expeditions. *Twister* created a second huge tape collection, but this time technology made it possible to create order out of the chaos. Kesey acquired state-of-the-art digital editing equipment, and he and Babbs, both then coming up on sixty, spent pretty much every night for three years learning how to use it to edit *Twister.* Out in the rainy Oregon dark, the lights glowed in the cookhouse or over in the bus barn vault. They laid out one master audio track and proceeded to edit fragments of everything else, audio and video, onto it. Whenever necessary they would summon cast members and restage a scene where a close-up was needed, or create and film some entire new bit that was called for. The editing was painstaking work, with endless setbacks, crashes, and failing drives, and it was sometimes painful to watch from my New York outpost. Video cassettes would bring me chunks of the ever-evolving film, and anecdotes tracked the roller-coaster progress. One dawn Babbs e-mailed to report that he'd just accidentally and irrevocably erased the entire second act. It had taken three months to edit. "Oh well. We'll redo it."

When the video came out, it sold briskly on the Prankster website. And editing *Twister* cleared the way for solving the mystery of the great Bus Movie. Kesey and Babbs had their chops down and could now tackle this epic. Thus began another years-long project. It necessitated a move from the farm to "the office," two rooms of a former motel a few miles down the road, conveniently next door to the local post office, from which Phil Dietz launched a steady stream of *Twister* videos. In rooms packed with computers and editing equipment and shelf after shelf of film and videotape, the great Bus Movie slowly took shape, Kesey, Babbs, and Phil at their posts in one room, Simon Babbs and Zane Kesey working away at their consoles in the other.

The bus movie, formally known as *Intrepid Traveler and His Merry Band of Pranksters Look for a Kool Place*, was a film within and about a film: Pranksters open up The Vault and fire up creaky old projectors that spark to life and project the original bus movie footage on the wall. The Pranksters watch and anecdotally annotate it, cutting in with still photos and new footage and other material. It was an elaborate creative process, with nights of shooting and months of editing, and progress slow but steady.

In 1998 Viking Penguin gave me my tenth-anniversary Tiffany clock, followed shortly by my walking papers. I hadn't brought in enough bestsellers. I spent too much time editing. I had an old-fashioned attitude. I didn't know how to "move product." All true. Kesey was on the phone immediately. Wherever I wanted to go, we'd go. I felt in my gut that I couldn't place my fate in the hands of another big publishing corporation, so I took the shove as an opportunity to leap, and went freelance. I would keep working with Kesey as his out-house editor. Our inside link would be our long-time friend and ally, Paul Slovak, now his in-house editor.

While the bus movie proceeded that winter Kesey and I started in on a multibook proposal for his longtime agent Sterling Lord to present to Viking. Despite my hard parting, it seemed best to try to keep his entire body of work in one place.

One of the books in the proposal would be the long-pondered autobiography, and it was the structure of the bus movie that had suggested the way to approach it. Starting from the present, Ken would narrate his way back through the journals. He came to refer to this as his "psortabiography."

But aside from Ken's periodic traveling around the country for teaching and speaking engagements, the bus movie was all-consuming. The instrument of its completion came via a deadline that was contained within yet another huge undertaking. In 1998 Kesey and Babbs went to London for a speaking tour, working with promoter Paul Smith in London. Out of this trip and this relationship came the plan for an ambitious bus tour of the UK, paid for by British TV's upstart Channel 4 as the centerpiece of their 1999 "Summer of Love" commemoration. The deal included the cost of shipping Further to the UK, and funding for a thirty-day tour of Kesey's new multimedia theatrical piece *WheresMerlin?* (written for the occasion) through England, Wales, Ireland, and Scotland. It also called for delivery of the finished first hour of the bus movie, which would have its world premiere on Channel 4.

Both tour and show were conceived as a quest for Merlin at the turn of the millennium, seeking some sign or insight from his spirit at an epochal moment of transition. Kesey's script drew heavily on classic texts and Arthurian legend. The all-Prankster cast featured Arthur, Gueneviere, Lancelot, Morgana, Queen Mab, Nimue, Modred, Sir Kay, a Fool, and even a Churl. There were witches and a steaming cauldron, a bevy of faeries, ornate oration, and for the denouement an elaborate nineteenth-century stage magic trick Chuck had found in a dusty tome. Costumes, throne, banners, and armor were all prepared with care, and after months of rehearsal all was bent for England.

The show would begin with Kesey doing magic—pulling fireflies out of Caleb's mouth. Then, donning a headscarf, he'd evoke Gramma Smith and the storytelling that had inspired him, calling up an audience member to help him recite the nursery rhyme that gave *Cuckoo's Nest* its name. Then came a reading of *Tricker*, an intermission, and on to *WheresMerlin?*, which began with John Swan's beautiful rendition of Yeats's *The Stolen Child*, and ended with a musical extravaganza built around "Love Potion No. 9" (Kesey thwamping away on the Thunder Machine as the skeleton "Mr. Bones"). The musical portion of the show would rev up for a while, then at some point Kesey would bring the music down low, or even stop it, and launch into spontaneous commentary on matters at hand. Then the music would kick back in and regain full momentum, Kesey wailing and howling away on his beloved Theramin until the end.

The UK trip was huge fun and hard work—setup, performance, breakdown, load, and ride. And advance publicity proved insufficient. We stumped for the show all over London, flashing the sign of the Day-Glo hand, stopping to play music from the roof of the bus and hand out flyers. Kesey, Babbs, and M.G. did radio interviews to bring in a crowd, and as we drove we broadcast our bus chatter and tunes, live from on board via FM station KBUZ. Are We Really? (aka Freddy Hahne) chronicled the trip daily on the Web. Channel 4 was often with us, and interspersed its reports among the "Summer of Love" documentaries.

In London promoter Paul Smith had arranged for us to go to the home of artist Ken Bright and his family. After a lovely and restorative backyard feast, Kesey was touring the house and saw a blank, primed 5' x 5' canvas hanging in Bright's studio. Soon it was laid out under the street lamps, and we'd hauled the art box off the bus and set to work on what turned out to be a pretty nice piece. For the final step, paint was artfully applied to the front right tire of Further, and Kesey climbed aboard and drove over the canvas. Voilá! The first Bus Painting was carried back into the house and rehung in its spot.

A few nights later Channel 4 threw a big Summer of Love party at the Institute for Contemporary Arts, not far from

Buckingham Palace. We rolled up, debarked, and found an elaborate event under way inside, complete with simulated '60s-style dance hall, throbbing lights, music, and slide projections. But drinks were expensive, the atmosphere was stiff, and Kesey seemed reluctant to spend the evening doing meet-and-greet with TV execs. So we went back to the bus, hauled the paint box out, and did another bus painting. Chuck did particularly nice work with leaves and spray paint. When it was finished, Kesey and Babbs carried it into the museum and ceremoniously presented it to the surprised director.

A few mornings later in Stratford-on-Avon we prepared to mount up for the day's ride while Kesey visited with two small children who'd journeyed with their parents many miles to meet him. The boys had painted a small toy bus of their own, and with great solemnity presented it to Kesey. This day was to take us from the home of the Bard to Liverpool, so we climbed on board and cranked up the Beatles. Eileen Babbs and I huddled under a blanket up top and sang along at the top of our lungs.

Liverpool was a revelation, not the gloomtown we expected somehow, but eye-rich with huge cathedrals and unusual architecture. High atop a downtown building great metal birds were poised for flight. With drum and drummers up top we rolled through bustling afternoon downtown traffic, and eased our way into a narrow alley which was packed with a crowd that burst into cheers. We'd arrived at The Cavern, the underground club where the Beatles so often played, and it was the most boisterous reception of the tour.

The next night *WheresMerlin?* drew a good crowd at the Royal Court Theatre, a venue the Beatles had played long ago. Instead of beginning with *Tricker,* Kesey read *Now We Know How Many Holes It Takes to Fill the Albert Hall,* his remarkable John Lennon piece. At my usual post behind the camera I clambered around throughout the great old hall filming from various angles, including way up at the back of the third balcony. For *WheresMerlin?* I crawled up from the basement and lodged myself in the orchestra pit for close-ups. Through the lens I saw everything so clearly. There was Kesey singing, so naked and passionate, as open and vulnerable as could be, giving himself completely to the moment. Behold the "Tarnished Galahad," his silver helmet gleaming with its weather vane and crowing rooster, slightly askew as he grins, sweat streaming down his face, and sings about Neal and the bus. "Coming, coming, coming around. . . . Coming around." And John Cassady, Neal's son, is playing guitar. And strands of smoke wind their way up and swirl around the stage. A Liverpudlian from the audience has climbed up and is pogo-ing around the stage. Another nods with the beat, playing serious air guitar next to Kesey, who shares a microphone with Swan. "The bus came by and I got on, that's when it all began. . . . There was cowboy Neal, at the wheel of a bus to nevereverland. . . . Coming, coming, coming around. . . . Coming around. Coming around . . ." and Kesey takes off from there, bringing the music down and launching into his rap. He introduces everyone in the band and the cast, then calls Faye out, introducing her with a hug. He's drenched in sweat, focused, grinning, and his eyes are shining bright. "With guns it didn't work . . . with bows and arrows. . . . It didn't work with rocks. . . . We have to change the human heart, right at the core. . . . We have to change it where it starts. . . . And we're not very many people. . . . And the only way that we can work is not to get pissed off about what's going on. . . . When you get pissed off about it, it's got you. . . . The Evil Force doesn't care which side you're on, whether you're for abortion or against abortion. It just wants you to be on either side. . . . Don't go for it. . . . Don't go for it. . . . When you feel that happening, reach out to the other person with all that you've got, all that you can muster. Reach out with your heart. . . . The only thing that will work is love . . . and it's coming around, coming around, coming around, again. . . . Reach out to each other now. . . . God bless the Beatles. God bless the Beatles. God bless the Beatles. . . ."

I had to get off the bus that night and head for home. As

Further and the caravan vanished in a cloud of sound, it was a strange and dismaying sensation. Where is everyone? For a long time, automobiles seemed ridiculously small.

Late in 1999 the bus movie, part one, was sent to England. Soon after, VHS cassettes began to flow out from the Pleasant Hill post office at a pace that quickened dramatically after a CNN story. Naturally each box was a handmade work of art, carefully "dipped" using a perfected floating oil paint technique. Hundreds would be done at once, all arrayed in the bus barn to dry. Kesey and Babbs would add stickers, voice-balloons, drawings, and their signatures. Editing of the bus movie, part two, subtitled *North to Madhattan*, began immediately.

Through 2000 Kesey's battle with hep C became increasingly serious and began to draw away his energy, though he continued to edit the film and work on the *Jail Journal*. I made periodic visits, including one at New Year's 2001, a chilly and rainy time at the farm. Faye was away. We went over the book proposal, now complete except for the psortabiography, and spent time in the vault with the journals. As fireworks filled the distant sky we threw the Ching, then watched *Pi* and *The Godfather*. He told me I should find one of Burt Lancaster's lesser-known films, *Rocket Gibraltar*, which was about a writer's last days.

In the morning we did some dictation. After his stroke in 1995 it had taken a while to get his hand strength back, and since I was a speed typist we'd tried storytelling sessions from time to time, using my laptop. Ken's writing and interview voices are different, but he spoke in complete sentences and it was easy to clean up a transcription. But as promising as this approach seemed for perhaps nailing down episodes Ken hadn't written about, he wasn't really a phone person, and with him in Oregon and me in New York we had managed to capture only a few bits.

In April he came out to Albany to speak as part of William Kennedy's Writers Voices program. The interferon treatment he was taking had battered him, but he directed all the energy he had at the students. He'd requested time for a good nap between his appearance at a class in the afternoon and the evening event, yet he lingered long to talk. Paul Slovak and I urged him out and along through the parking lot, but he spotted a bus one group of students had ridden on from Pennsylvania, and climbed on board to admire the vehicle, giving them advice on alterations.

At the show that night Ken brought the audience inside his situation, forewarning them that he would occasionally forget what he was saying. Whenever it happened the audience cheerfully narrated him back on track. There was a warm and jovial dinner with Kennedy and his family and friends that night after the program.

Ken was coming to our house in Amenia for a few days, and en route from Albany next morning I took a wrong turn and found myself unable to get off the Mass Pike. Ken was asleep, and as we drove in sunny silence, imprisoned on the toll road for much of an hour, I couldn't tell for certain if he was breathing. He was so pale, and had seemed so shaky, and I was worried. But as we finally escaped from the big road and started to wind our way south he roused. A call to Faye told him recent tests showed the interferon wasn't working, and he stopped taking it. His color soon began to come back.

Therese and I hadn't had Kesey with us since Hoboken. Now we were renting a house on a farm 100 miles north. Dairy cows reached through the barbed wire to nibble our yard. Ken perched on the picnic table, looking out over the Smithfield Valley. The bird songs were different, he said. And the frogs. And the plants. We sat in my summer office, a table up on the hill, and did some more dictation, watching the kids—Grace, Harry, and Sophia—play in the yard. We ironed out the description of the psortabiography, so we could take the completed proposal down to Sterling in the city and give it to him, then all go see Gary Sinise's Broadway production of *Cuckoo's Nest*. At night we talked while the cicadas churled away. Ken thought he was nearing the end of his run. Maybe a couple years more. We needed to get going on these projects when his strength returned. Getting Viking on board with the deal would spark us.

At bedtime he read to the children—*Little Tricker.* "Not in his big voice, just regular," recalls Grace. He'd been taking in our little scene, and out in the yard on the last day he announced his conclusion: "What you kids need is a tent." Down the hill we went to Ames, the town's big all-purpose store, and Kesey led the way to the camping goods department and told them to pick one out. "This is your tent," he instructed them. "It's just for you. You don't have to let any grown-ups in."

A few weeks later Kesey's liver cancer was diagnosed. After surgery in October signs were initially good, but his situation deteriorated. When I got to Eugene, Faye ran back through the entire sequence of his weeks-long struggle in profound detail and with utter clarity. Logic indicated he was at the end. Still, I couldn't help hoping that with his great strength he would reach down deep inside and somehow manage to pull himself out of the hat. But it was not to be. "Hard times call for strong rituals," he said many times, advice borne out by the sorrow and glory of his burial.

Over a year later *Kesey's Jail Journal* was turned in to Paul Slovak at Viking Penguin. On his visit to Amenia, Ken had brought me disks of the text. Printing them all out I realized there were several overlapping versions. "File management wasn't his strong point," noted Babbs. Out at the farm in January 2003 I worked through the various versions and merged them into a master, adding in some pieces he had left, following his instructions, some written, some remembered. During these quiet rainy days I had the book and all the original art panels spread out upstairs. Faye would work downstairs preparing for her Bible study teaching. Happy the wonderdog padded upstairs and down between both work stations, staring out various windows as the rain pattered down. In the evenings Faye and I mulled over various editorial questions, as we would continue to do by phone in the months that followed.

Most of the books Kesey had included in the multivolume

proposal are not possible without Kesey. But the *Jail Journal*, at least, is complete. Early one Sunday I went out to his grave. As I stood beside it in the glory of the morning a goose flew in low, honking, across the pasture. As I looked up it swept past, a few feet above my head, and I heard the air move.

HORNSWOGGLED

By Ken Babbs

We were going down to the swamp to split some wood. He looked me over.

"You've got your gloves, don't you?"

"You kidding? I don't take a leak without putting on my gloves."

"If I had a dick like that I'd wear gloves too."

Ha ha. He was always pulling one on me. We arrived at the pile we'd bucked up the day before. He used a wedge and sledge. I was a maul man. He set the wedge and pecked at it with his sledge until the round of wood split down the middle. Then he split each piece in two the same way.

I set a round up and lifted the maul high over my head and brought it down hard enough to split the round in half with one whack. If the wood was straight-grained. Twisted, it took more than one whack. Sometimes a lot more.

He reached back with his sledge, getting another round, and swung the nine-pound head close to me.

"Watch it," I said. "You're liable to squash my balls with that thing."

"I didn't think you wanted any more kids anyway," he said.

Har har. I let it pass and we started in again. After a while he said, "You know, you'd save a lot of energy using a wedge and sledge instead of that maul."

"Yeah, but it would take twice as long."

"Twice as long as what? You're not going any faster than I am."

"You kidding me? There's no way you can split wood with a wedge and sledge faster than I can with a maul."

"You want to bet?"

"Does a fox suck eggs? Name your wager and make it easy on yourself."

"I'll go twenty bucks for twenty minutes."

"You're on."

He nodded and we set in. I grabbed those rounds and started whacking for all I was worth. I could hear him hitting at a steady beat. This was going to be a cinch. After a while I had to take off my sweatshirt. His forehead wasn't even damp. Pretty soon I was glancing at my watch. The twenty minutes were starting to drag. But I wasn't about to let up. I pushed it right to the end.

"That's it," I said. "Time's up."

He stepped back and surveyed the pile. "Well," he said. "I guess you hornswoggled me this time."

You bet I had. It wasn't even close. We'd split that whole pile and he hadn't done piddling. The wood around me was high as my waist. His came up to his ankles.

"Well come on," he said. "Let's throw the wood in the truck. We've got time to go down to Jim's Landing and have a drink. You can buy."

The flush of victory lasted about two minutes. It took me that long to realize I'd been hornswoggled again. He didn't rub it in though. It might make me more wary the next time.

GETTING BETTER

A Radio Interview Conducted by Sharon Wood, with John Nance and Paul Pintarich

> *The friends that have it I do wrong*
> *Whenever I remake a song*
> *Should know what issue is at stake,*
> *It is myself that I remake.*
> —*The Collected Works in Verse and Prose of William Butler Yeats* [1908], II, preliminary poem

July 30, 1986. I met writers John Nance and Paul Pintarich in Portland in the late afternoon, and Nance drove us the 115 miles down to Springfield to interview Ken Kesey, Oregon's most famous novelist. *Demon Box*, a collection of Kesey's essays, had just been published by Viking, and was already being delivered to Oregon bookstores. To promote the book, he was preparing his "Still Kesey" tour, with New York the ultimate destination.

The interview was to air on KBOO, the independent Portland FM station, on a program called "Between the Covers: Interviews with Northwest Writers," of which I was the original host. Nance, author of *The Mud Pie Dilemma* and *The Gentle Tasaday: A Stone Age People in the Philippine Rain Forest*, both published in the 1970s, was also an award-winning photographer; he had graduated with Kesey from the University of Oregon. Pintarich, books editor for the Portland *Oregonian*, was along to ask questions for a column about *Demon Box*. Our interview took place on the back porch of the Kesey home, just outside Pleasant Hill, a tiny farming community (pop. 75) located two miles below the Dexter Dam on the Willamette River.

The sun had warmed the heart of the Willamette Valley to 81 degrees that afternoon. The long, narrow porch, just wide enough to contain the recording equipment and the four of us, was on the field side of the kitchen's sliding glass door. We looked out to grape arbor, tomatoes, pond, pasture—wheel and hub of an eighty-acre farm and dairy worked by the second and third Kesey generations. Dairy cows stood in the next field, with sheep not far off. Roosters and nervous hens groused at our feet. Owls, we were told, roosted in the far rafters of the house, which, greatly remodeled, had been the farm's original barn; Kesey allowed the stoic birds inside. The fowl that took front and center that evening, however, was the family parrot, Rumiocho, distinctive for his piercing whistle and his devotion to Kesey.

Ken and Faye Kesey's second son, Jed, had died in January 1984, not two full grieving seasons prior to our visit. The Keseys had buried the twenty-year-old in a family-made pine coffin about two hundred feet from the kitchen sliding-glass door, on a hill gently rising between the chicken coop and a big egg-shaped pond.

I had read the dedication page of *Demon Box* during the drive down from Portland: "To Jed / across the river / riding point."

As we prepared to begin the interview, Ken and Faye's first-born son, Zane, tinkered with the "Thunder Machine," a large handmade music-making thingamajig the elder Kesey uses in his performances. With a shotgun angled out the front, and a volcano, fired by CO_2, pluming from the top, the Thunder Machine—wired for digital leads—could have been fashioned by

Dr. Seuss. Faye, married to Kesey all the days and nights since 1954, was inside cooking dinner. During our stay, many visitors opened but didn't always close the front door of the Kesey home.

As to the man himself, what was left of his blond curls was six weeks past a haircut. He wore a t-shirt and blue jeans, the former not new and the latter with hardened work-dirt on both knees.

(Later, after our interview, he would reappear looking like one of the Blues Brothers, in full regalia for a dress rehearsal of the "Still Kesey" band out in the pasture. As part of the promotion for the coming tour, John Nance was to photograph the rehearsal for the Portland *Oregonian*.)

In the late afternoon sky a faint crescent moon was already gearing up to hang loose, as I pushed "play" and "record."

—SWW

Sharon Wood: Where did the title *Demon Box* come from?

Ken Kesey: It's based on a notion a guy named Clark Maxwell had a hundred years ago about—oh, it's too hard to explain real quick here, but it has to do with our minds. In our minds we have this little box, and on one side of the box is the good and on the other side of the box is the bad, and the effort to sort the good from the bad is costing more than we're getting, and I use this metaphor loosely through the book to try to shed some light on the psychedelic movement of the '60s.

Paul Pintarich: It is fiction, isn't it? Fictional essays? Or how would you describe it?

KK: It's one of those things, as you read it, you can tell a lot of it is real stuff that I've kept notes on, but I have bent it to fit into the themes of the book, so it's fiction.

PP: What period does this represent?

KK: This is the '70s and into the '80s, a fifteen-year period writing it.

John Nance: I understand you to say you're really focusing on the '60s psychedelic . . . Is there something more you want to say about that?

KK: This is what I talk about, the "come-down" years. This [*Demon Box*] isn't about the '60s. It's after the '60s. The stories all start in 1969, which I really feel like was the time when things began to fall apart. You remember "Alice's Restaurant," you remember the other side of "Alice's Restaurant" when he's singing, "I don't want a pickle, I just wanna ride my motorcycle"? Remember, he's riding along on his motorcycle and he goes over a cliff, and as he's going over the cliff, he sings [Kesey sings], "I don't want to die, just want to ride on my motor-sigh-cul." And he says, "I knew it wasn't the best thing I ever wrote, but it was the best thing I could do coming down." And that's the way I feel about it. It's not the best thing I ever wrote, but all my Kentucky writer friends told me, "Son, you've been in the field for twenty years. We need you to report, never mind literature."

PP: A lot of people have asked me, and I'm sure they've asked you, if maybe when you wrote *Sometimes a Great Notion*—which a lot of us consider a minor masterpiece—if that might have been writing out everything.

KK: Well, how many no-hitters can you pitch in the major leagues? I doubt that I will ever equal *Notion*. I don't think I have the capacity. I don't think I have the energy, or the concentration to do it, and I don't feel bad about that, except that when I talk to American writers—and one of the great things about being famous is you get to talk with other famous people, so I've had Norman Mailer here, and I've had

Arthur Miller, and had a chance to talk to Richard Hugo and people like that—and one of the things we always talk about is what happens to American writers. Why don't we get any better?

JN: But that idea you had, I mean, particularly following *Cuckoo's Nest*, we're talking about a boom-boom kind of effect there, very powerful. I've often wondered myself what that meant to you, I mean, two such resounding successes, one after the other?

KK: Well, I've never had any doubt as to who I was. That's never bothered me.

PP: Don't you have an Alaska book somewhere that you are trying to finish?

KK: Oh, yeah, I've got three hundred pages of this written, but here's what happened, see. I was working hard on this, I was deep into it, but I found that the Gonzo, the Kesey persona, had so much interrupted that book that I couldn't do what Larry is doing in *Lonesome Dove*. And I know writing well enough to know that, you know, you can feel it that when Larry takes out on that book it is as much an adventure for him as a writer as it is for you as a reader. . . . Have you read the Hemingway book? [*The Garden of Eden*, Scribner's 1986]. A sad book. It's a good book if it had come out in the '30s. But coming out now, it's wrong. This is what scares me.

JN: What is the wrongness of that, and how would you describe it?

KK: Well, you're talking about women with short hair and in slacks, and that had a certain hit then, and if it had been published then it would have had that hit. Now, it doesn't have that hit. It's a different hit.

PP: But it is a hit as far as reflecting on his personality. It says a lot about him, that he could never say.

KK: But that's not what a writer wants to do, really. I mean, Shakespeare doesn't say anything about Shakespeare. I'm tired of saying stuff about Kesey. I mean that becomes finally almost an industry.

JN: If Shakespeare were to write today, could he step back from being Shakespeare? With that kind of exposure—you know, he would have to go out selling books, hyping—could he have pulled back and been allowed himself to be just old Bill Shakespeare, cranking out something back there . . . ?

KK: It would have been harder for him because, you know, there'd have been Baba Wawa wanting him on television.

JN: Did he have to go, though?

KK: Well, you don't like to be impolite. When people ask you a question you assume that they ask you because you know [the answer]. I mean, if somebody asks me the weight of Mars, they assume I know, and I try to make something up. And this is what a fiction writer does. And pretty soon you're caught. That was not something that Shakespeare had to deal with.

SW: You talk about your twilight years. How old are you?

KK: Seventy-nine, eighty.

JN: At least eighty-two.

KK: I'm talking about working talent. I'm talking about Muhammad Ali. I'm talking about when you can deliver a punch. And move correctly.

JN: There's a certain pacing about that, I mean, you can come out and maybe save yourself for the ninth round to the twelfth, [but] in between you've really got to know what's in there . . .

KK: I don't feel like this—I hope—this isn't my [last] book. I got books in me yet.

PP: Long ones?

KK: I don't know if I've got long ones. I don't know if I've got another *Notion* in me. I saw a kid win the World Juggling contest on television last week. He juggled twelve Indian clubs. Now, I know the Flying Karamazov Brothers [a popular troupe of acrobats]. There's none of them can do that. This kid is probably fourteen, sixteen. Maybe you can only do that a certain time. Now, when I was doing *Notion*, I had more balls in the air than I can keep in the air right now.

JN: I wondered how much of that is really conscious, or [does it] just kind of flow through you? Could you have calculated that, or was it just happening?

KK: Oh, I'm a professional. Yeah, I know what I'm doing. And I'm doing it as full-out as I can, all the time. I got the metal to the floor all the time.

JN: You refer also to some kind of power other than your own. Are you conscious of that when you're writing, or are some of the words just coming out?

KK: Well, we're now talking about muses. "Muse," as Wendell Berry says, comes from musing on something, from reflecting and thinking on something. And we went through a period of time in which we were taken by the muse without having to reflect [that] it was moving us.

To get back to this thing about American writers, and

what it is about American writers: You know when I talk with Mailer, Miller and Vonnegut, Wendell Berry and Larry McMurtry, about who got better in writing, you know who is the only person they can agree on that got better? Now, think about the last hundred years or so, who got better? Yeats. Yeats got better, and he was writing good stuff at eighty.

PP: How about Joyce?

KK: Well, I don't know that he got better. I think he got more willful.

PP: How about Henry Miller? Do you like Henry Miller?

KK: I love Henry Miller, but I don't think he got better. I don't think Faulkner got better. I don't think Hemingway got better. I don't think Steinbeck got better. Styron, none of those people. They hit their stride at a certain time and from there on glided to the grave.

PP: Do you write poetry?

KK: Lots. I like the Robert Graves thing, that poetry is the language we speak through the ages. I have a real sense of my talent and I know where I stand amongst people, and I know how good I am and how good I ought to be, and I ought to be better. And that rubs you somewhat, but when you're courting the muses and you really want to be touched by moving spirits, you find you can't do it in New York, you can't do it in Hollywood. Even if I'm not writing, I'm closer to it out in that field than I am when I'm back in New York. Now, with this book coming out, I tell you the thing that really made the difference to me was I have taken these stories and these pieces of stuff back to New York a number of times. These pieces have been available to Viking for ten years. Why haven't they published them? Why haven't they seen them as a work? It's because they are trying to go with the gusto. There's a certain amount of media movement . . .

JN: Marketing.

KK: Marketing, and if I'm trying to sell those cows, I don't take those cows and drive them to New York. I bring the people from New York out to look at the cows.

So I got an editor, finally, and I haven't had an editor in ten years. I mean, Viking has changed hands three times, I've had five editors, I've had all of these people who I've finally convinced that I'm trying to do something, and then they change houses, or the house changes hands. They move, and so, finally, I've got this guy, Chuck Verrill, who really came to me by way of Gurney Norman, my old buddy from the great writing class at Stanford.

JN: McMurtry—was he in that class?

KK: McMurtry was in that class, Wendell Berry was in that class, Ernie Gaines, Peter Beagle . . . Malcolm Cowley taught it. [Note: Here Kesey, who attended writing classes at Stanford off and on over a three-year period, is conflating the class of '58–'59 and the class of '60–'61. The former was taught by Wallace Stegner and Richard Scowcroft, the latter by Cowley and Frank O'Connor.] This is the famous writing class at Stanford. All of the people that came out of it have done well, and I've tried to understand why a number of times, and I think it goes back to Malcolm Cowley. Malcolm Cowley taught us something about writing which has to do with more than writing. It has to do with respect for writing, and respect for people who have written. Whenever I do a writing seminar, the first thing I tell them is that it's just as hard to write a bad novel as it is a good novel, and that you don't ever want to hurt anybody, and that when somebody publishes something good, every writer triumphs, and so it's not a competition. It's like throwing the javelin. You're not throwing the javelin against Petronov. You're throwing the javelin against distance and weight.

PP: Do you consider yourself a regional or Northwest writer?

KK: Yeah, I do. Very much. You gotta work out of where your feet fit the ground . . .

PP: And overwhelming the landscape seems quite a challenge, too, for the writers here.

KK: You can see what I've been doing with that Thunder Machine out there. You can see what I'm doing with this reading [series]. I'm moving off the page, back out in front of people, back around the campfire, and when I talk to writers, or when I talk to musicians, or when I talk to filmmakers, I have to overcome the fact that they're writers, or musicians, or filmmakers. I'm not interested in all of that stuff. I'm interested in only one thing, and that's the magic of it. You use whatever you can to make it go . . .

PP: Are we talking about storytelling?

KK: Storytelling, and opera, and rock and roll . . .

PP: In other words, performing.

JN: But this again puts the writer out there, as opposed to Shakespeare—puts you onstage. I can recall even at Oregon at the Spring Competition, I mean, you were out there, singing and leading and writing things and so on, and that's one of the things I remembered about that time, that you were out there as a writer, but also as director, performer, and there was something about your personality that seemed to be drawn to that, and you did it extremely well.

KK: Yeah, well, I think that was what the writer *was* before Gutenberg. The show that went from castle to castle, trying to keep civilization together by telling how beautiful the women were in the other cave, and how the strong men killed the dragon. That to me is what you're judged by. You walk out into an arena, and it's relatively easy to draw the spotlight, that's the thing a lot of people don't understand. My dad used to say about me, he says, "You can draw a crowd in the desert!" But what do you do with the crowd, once you're drawn 'em? Can you tell them the truth? That's the thing. Can you stand shoulder to shoulder with people you respect through the ages, you know, the Baal ShemTov of Hasidic literature? Can you stand up there with Rimbaud? Can you stand up there with Faulkner? These are really our allies in an ongoing revolution fighting against a deadly thing in our nation today.

JN: Which is?

KK: It's growing fascism.

JN: I was going to ask you about evil.

KK: Melville, man, *Moby Dick* is the book. It has to do with there is something there that we have to combat all the time. . . . And it isn't necessarily a human being. It takes the form of a human being now and then, but it also may be a whale and may be something inside of you. It is ever present, but it's off of evil. It's . . . this is the thing about *Cuckoo's Nest:* People think that the big nurse is the villain. She is not the villain. She is a minion of the villain, but she is not the villain. The villain is something else. If you reduce it to her being the villain, it loses its importance. So what's important is finding what the villain is.

SW: What is the job of the writer?

KK: Well, the truth is the job of the writer. You know, people keep getting truth mixed up with what is true. If you're sitting there and you see two guys with long hair-locks and black hats run over and hide in that grape arbor right there, and the Gestapo runs up behind them with a gun and says, "Have you seen two Jews hide in there?" What's the truth? The truth is, 'No, they ran up on the road." So the truth is something that can't be pinned down arbitrarily. It has to be something that the soul and the heart seeks out. The job of the writer is to get down there in the trenches and fight for the soul of the people, and say, "The truth is . . ."

PP: Look at the old beatniks. They were gentle, loving, truly open people—and they were brought suddenly into the world of *Miami Vice.*

KK: The beatniks were tougher than the hippies. They held on, but the old hippies, they didn't.

SW: How old are you, Ken?

KK: Fifty. You finally—you watch what happens. Like this barn: This barn was built by the old man down the road here. He still brings in all of his grain, he cracks all of his grain, all the grain that we buy to feed our chickens here comes from him. He built this barn, he and his family and his in-laws, in a week. It's still there. It's hard, it's strong, it's true, it's laid out north and south and east and west, it's still pure and clean, and a hundred years after other things fall, even if this barn is just a tiny structure, it will still be talking about what this old man felt in the past.

PP: Will you still be here? You gonna live here and keep farming?

KK: I got a kid buried on this land. They'd have to root me out with a bulldozer. . . . [Somewhere nearby, a dog barks, growls, barks again.] Hear that dog a-growlin' and a-barkin'? Yeah! [Laughs.]

The *"Still Kesey"* band—performing here in an open pasture behind the Kesey house for an audience largely consisting of several astonished cows—included, in addition to Ken, John Swan (stand-up bass), Zane Kesey (Thunder Machine), and Art Maddox (keyboard).

AN UNHEARD MELODY

Photo Essay by John Nance

*Heard melodies are sweet, but those unheard
Are sweeter . . .*
      —Keats, "Ode on a Grecian Urn"

Robert Hunter, the poet, musician, and Grateful Dead lyricist, became a friend of Kesey's in the Perry Lane days. His collected lyrics is titled A Box of Rain.

LAMENT FOR KESEY

By Robert Hunter

all away all away all away all
draggin 'em all away
down into down with
a scream or a sigh
a smile and a nod,
quiet or in full cry
here comes Death
draggin 'em all away

sneak around corners
up out of grates
eagles and the ants,
spiders and the cormorants,
draggin 'em all away

Damn you Death,
I piss on your shoes,
Father of Blues
get offa my land
or I'll run you through!

And who'll be there to
get you when I do?

Never could say goodbye
like it had any kind
of final rectitude,
any essential rightness.
Whatever's right, yeah?
Whatever's true—
later, not farewell.
As in, see you around.

Death is senseless
unless we just pop over
into some other place,
along with the eagles and ants,
the spiders and cormorants,
the destitute and shameless,
the brightest and best—
born to be banished
banished to be born.

One stood in the moonlight
One stood out in the crowd
One stood under star blue sky
his daydream turned up loud.

How did this come to pass?
Don't gimme no don't gimme no . . .
this tractor don't run on horseshit,
Deboree, just natural gas.

Some folk come
to stir it up
and when it's stirred
they split—simple as that

—11/10/01

244

Brer Kesey's Words to the Wise

Fame is a wart.

Speak swiftly, and carry a big soft.

A vote for Barry is a vote for fun.

The answer is never the answer.
The need for mystery is always greater
than the need for answers.

If you've got it all together, what's that all
around it?

Nepotism is better than no potism at all.

I'm pushed by the pump and pulled
by the plow.

It's true even if it didn't happen.

The only real currency is the currency of the
spirit.

When you don't know where you're
going, you have to stick together just
in case someone gets there.

You can't make an opera out of Johnny
Fuckerfaster. (George Walker: No,
it's more of a ballet.)

Ach du Libra, said the zebra.

Always stay in your own movie.

Nothing lasts.

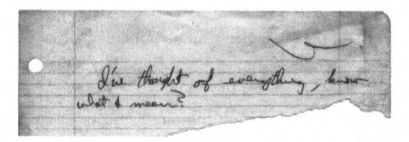

—KK, circa 1966